The Girls' Guide to DREAMS

Kristi Collier-Thompson

Illustrated by
Sandie Turchyn

Sterling Publishing Co., Inc., New York

To Trent, the star of my dreams, and

To Samantha, follow yours.

Library of Congress Cataloging-in-Publication Data

10 9 8 7 6 5 4 3 2 1

Thompson, Kristi Collier.
  The girls' guide to dreams / Kristi Collier Thompson ; illustrated by
Sandie Turchyn.
       p. cm.
  Summary: Introduces how to interpret the symbols often found in dreams
and to apply what can be learned from them to events in one's waking
life, and includes directions for keeping a dream journal.
  Includes index.
  1. Children's dreams–Juvenile literature. 2. Dream
interpretation–Dictionaries–Juvenile literature. 3. Symbolism
(Psychology)–Dictionaries–Juvenile literature. [1. Dreams. 2.
Symbolism (Psychology)–Dictionaries.] I. Turchyn, Sandie, ill. II.
Title.
BF1099.C55T46 2003
154.6'3'08352–dc21
Edited by Nancy E. Sherman

Published by Sterling Publishing Co., Inc.
387 Park Avenue South, New York, NY 10016
© 2003 by Kristi Collier-Thompson
Distributed in Canada by Sterling Publishing
c/o Canadian Manda Group, One Atlantic Avenue, Suite 105
Toronto, Ontario, Canada M6K 3E7
Distributed in Great Britain and Europe by Chris Lloyd at Orca Book
Services, Stanley House, Fleets Lane, Poole BH15 3AJ, England
Distributed in Australia by Capricorn Link (Australia) Pty. Ltd.
P.O. Box 704, Windsor, NSW 2756, Australia

Sterling ISBN 1-4027-0032-6

Contents

Introduction

EVER WAKE UP and wonder, "Why did I dream that?" Dreams often seem to make no sense at all. You may be tempted to forget all about your dream or to conclude that you will never be able to figure out what it means. Don't.

Dreams, however weird and wacky they may seem, often reveal important clues to your innermost secrets and thoughts. The stories your mind creates in the night often hold the keys to self-knowledge, happiness and sometimes, glimpses into the future.

Everybody dreams every night. You may not remember those dreams upon awakening, but that doesn't mean you don't dream. You may just not be aware. In fact, if you sleep for eight hours, two of them are spent dreaming. That's your own private movie premiere every night!

Dreams occur in cycles based on sleep patterns. The first dream begins after about ninety minutes of sleep and lasts about ten minutes. The cycles recur in ninety-minute segments, and the dreams get longer each time. The last dream may be as long as fifty minutes. This is generally the dream that is easiest to remember.

So what are dreams? Scientists aren't exactly sure why we need to sleep and it is less clear why we need to dream. But one thing is certain: dreams are necessary to maintain mental and physical health. In fact, people who are awakened before their dream cycles start and are thus prevented from dreaming tend to become anxious, insecure, and unsocial; not dreaming can also cause problems with learning and memory. Dreaming is important.

People have been interested in interpreting dreams since practically forever. The biblical book of *Genesis* tells how Joseph interpreted the dream of the Pharaoh and saved Egypt from starvation. Egyptian priests recorded the first known dream dictionary in 2000 B.C. A book considered the forerunner of modern dream dictionaries, *The Oneirocritica*, was written by an Italian physician named Artemidorus Daldianus in 200 A.D.

Dr. Sigmund Freud was the first modern medical professional to take dreams seriously. He published *The Interpretation of Dreams* in 1900. Freud theorized that dreams brought disturbing urges and wishes—things too unpleasant to face or think about directly—from the hidden unconscious into awareness through the use of symbols. His theories, while groundbreaking, were based on limited experience because he fully psychoanalyzed relatively few people.

Dr. Carl G. Jung built on Freud's foundation, analyzing his own dreams and thousands of those from a wide variety of clients. C.G. Jung developed a number of theories, among them the ideas of a deep-rooted inborn knowledge shared by everyone (called the collective unconscious) and instinctive symbols or patterns shared by everyone (known as archetypes). Jung believed that dream symbols do more than simply disguise things—they offer more comprehensive insights. Many of Jung's dream interpretations are still used today.

Consider the mind as an extraordinary computer that processes bits of information downloaded by the senses—everything you hear, eat, see, smell, feel. The computer is always running, but it needs downtime to process the data input during the day. Dreams help the mind do this. That's why seemingly unrelated or insignificant events, people, or things from your recent waking experience may appear in your dreams.

The unconscious is a powerful instrument; it keeps track of thoughts, feelings, and experiences. This unconscious material is constantly influencing your everyday life. Have you ever done something "on instinct" and later been unable to explain why you did it? Your unconscious was acting. Your dreams bring this unconscious activity to the surface. No matter how crazy a dream may appear, if you begin to examine the symbols in it and consider how the dream may parallel your waking life, you will begin to learn more about yourself, your hopes, your goals, your fears, and your roadblocks. Through your dreams you can tap into the wisdom and insight offered by your unconscious.

The dream exercises in this book will help you begin to understand how to identify the symbols in your dreams and then how to link them to what your unconscious mind may be trying to tell you. This dream dictionary contains the more common dream symbols and their possible meanings, but remember— the dream symbol is yours and yours alone. It may mean something entirely different to you than it does to your best friend. For example, a dream about a softball game may mean one thing to a star pitcher who is preparing for the tournament championship, another thing to someone who was hit in the eye with a softball, and something else again to someone who is always chosen last in gym class. Use the definitions here as a starting point from which to develop your own individual interpretations.

As you begin to study your dreams, you will find that you remember them more easily and that they begin to make more sense. Your ability to understand yourself and others will increase. So turn out the lights, close your eyes, and get to work!

Sweet dreams!

a

Abandonment (*See also* **Rejection**.)

If you dream about being abandoned, left behind, or forgotten, you may be feeling unwanted or unappreciated. Are you in a friendship that is failing? Do you feel that someone is letting you down? Or maybe, deep down, you don't really feel a part of the crowd. Take a good look at your relationships with family and friends. Does anything there trouble you? Abandonment dreams may likewise indicate that you are ready to abandon something—a relationship, an experience, an activity—and move on to things new and different.

Abnormal/Abnormality

In a dream, an abnormality may be some part of yourself, some feature that makes you uncomfortable or unhappy; once accepted though, it may actually bring you good fortune. The "deformity" may be what you most need to accept in yourself.

Accident

Accident dreams may be urging you to pay attention to something important—perhaps some risky behavior—that could lead to trouble. Take note of parallels in your everyday life. Some accident dreams are a way of dealing with the grief and emotional upheaval caused by a real-life accident.

Acid

It may be that something is "eating away" at you. Is there something you should be dealing with but keep putting aside? This unresolved issue may go sour and show up in your dreams.

Acne

Facial blemishes and distortions that plague you in your dreams often tap into everyday concerns, perhaps about your personal appearance or about leaving a wrong impression. You may be anticipating an event. Skin eruptions may also mean that you are dealing with hidden emotional turmoil or facing an outbreak of stress.

Acrobat

Acrobats tumbling through your dreams may symbolize trying a new approach, doing things differently. If you are dealing with a crisis, this dream may be suggesting that you respond not in the usual way (if you are typically laid back, you may need to be more assertive; if normally hyper, you may need to calm down).

Actor (*See also* **Audience**.)

Are you pretending to be something you're not? This dream may be telling you to take off the mask. It may also mean that you are hogging the spotlight or that you enjoy being the center of attention.

Adoption

This dream deals with feelings about family, belonging, being accepted, and finding wholeness.

Aging (*See also* **Wise Old Man/ Wise Old Woman**.)

A dream about growing older may deal with feelings about increasing maturity and responsibility or, alternatively, about leaving childhood and taking on new demands.

Air (*See also* **Flying**.)

Creativity, light, flight, freedom, and imagination are all related to air dreams. You may feel optimistic about your future or be on the verge of a great new idea or insight. Fresh, sweet-smelling air may mean you are ready for new opportunities. Muggy or polluted air generally has the opposite meaning. Explore what has you feeling negative.

Airplane

Airplanes are symbols of new ideas and insights. Dreaming of flying in an airplane may mean that you crave ambition and success. Perhaps you are gearing up to take a journey or have just returned from one. Consider how you feel about flying and airplanes.

Alarm Clock

This dream could be a wake-up notice—something needs to be done immediately. Have you been procrastinating? This could be your unconscious telling you to wake up and get to work. If you've been ignoring something serious, this may be a warning. Or it could be reactive—perhaps your real-life alarm clock is going off and you're just too sleepy to realize it!

Alien

See **Extraterrestrial**.

Alligator

Alligators may look slow and complacent, but they are vicious and quick to strike. Is there anything like that in your life? Are you consumed by schoolwork, a friendship, or an activity? Could this be the way you tend to behave?

Allowance

Dreaming about an increase or decrease in your allowance may be wish fulfillment (you wish your

✳ Alarm Clock ✳

parents would give you more money). Or, like other dreams about **Money**, it may mean that you are about to discover or have just discovered new and positive qualities within yourself. Money often represents your feelings of self-worth and self-esteem and the richness of your unique personality.

Amputation (*See also* **Operation**.)

This dream may reflect fear of losing something important to you or be inviting you to discard something that you no longer need. What is being amputated? What role does that part play in everyday life?

Anchor

An anchor is salvation, hope, safety, and help in danger. A dream of being anchored may indicate a desire for security in the midst of turmoil or stress. Alternatively, it may represent something that is holding you back or preventing you from moving toward your goals.

Angel

Angels may serve as messengers or guardians. Consider what the angel in your dream is doing or telling you. It may be sending a warning, an assurance of safety, or an important message or assignment.

Animal (*See also* **Wild Animal**.)

The type of animal in the dream is important (*see* **Exercise 5: Dream Animals**), likewise its behavior and actions. Animals often represent the wild, natural, uninhibited aspects of a person. Look carefully at what the creature symbolizes— were you ever bitten or traumatized by such an animal? Do you have a pet like the dream animal? It may alternatively signify something about yourself that you need to work on or some quality that you hope to acquire.

Ant

Ants are hardworking, highly organized creatures that work effectively together; they symbolize well-coordinated activity or teamwork. But dreaming of ants may also point to hyperactivity, nervousness, or fear of insignificance.

Antelope

The antelope symbolizes freedom, grace, and speed. It may signify overconfidence or being easily startled; as it bounds quickly into the forest, it may get entangled and become easy prey.

Ape

Apes are mimics, and dreaming of one may mean that you aren't thinking independently or are conforming too much to the crowd. Dream apes may suggest that you are acting irresponsible or childish. Apes also represent instinct—the intuitive side.

Apple
The apple symbolizes completeness and totality, and health, nature, the renewal of life, and immortality. But the dream apple may also caution against doing something foolish or forbidden.

Arrow (*See also* **Target**.)
The arrow in your dream may be pointing you toward a goal. Have you lost direction? This dream may be trying to give you focus and a target for which to shoot. The arrow may also represent anger or verbal hostility (barbs).

Attic (*See also* **House**.)
Every room in a house symbolizes something different, but they all refer generally to some part of your self. Attics may represent the head or mind. What is taking place there? Maybe you have thoughts or attitudes you haven't expressed. Are you holding them in storage, along with memories or forgotten goals and dreams?

B

Baby (*See also* **Child**.)
A baby in your dream may represent a part of you that feels frightened, immature, or helpless. An infant may express a wish to avoid grown-up responsibilities or problems; it may signify an activity or friendship that is just getting started.

Backpack
The contents of the backpack may be a clue to the dream's meaning. Do you have an emotional burden or problem that is weighing on you? The backpack may represent an extension of school. Or it may indicate an outdoor adventure.

Baking
See **Cooking**.

Balcony
Dreaming of being serenaded on a balcony suggests love and romance (as in *Romeo and Juliet*). If someone on the balcony is talking down to you, the dream balcony could be a symbol of unwanted authority or a feeling of being controlled.

Baldness (*See also* **Hair**.)
Hair often represents energy, strength, and beauty. Dreaming of

losing your hair may symbolize looking foolish, being taken advantage of, losing friendship, or not thinking clearly. Going bald may also suggest feelings of guilt, regret, or failure.

Ball (playing)

Do you have a big game coming up? Playing ball in your dream may be a way to practice for it mentally and to relieve anxiety. Playing ball also represents fun, freedom, and self-expression, unless you have always dreaded ball games, in which case it may release a fear. The ball itself may signify the earth, as well as wholeness and completeness.

Banana

Some regard the banana as a wisdom food, but most associate it with silliness and nonsense (monkeys and slipping on banana peels). Have you been playing practical jokes, or do you need more wackiness in your life?

Band

Parading or performing for others may point to a masking of your true self in pursuit of appreciation and applause. Alternatively, the parts of your personality may be creating harmony as they mature and come together. Your dream may be a mental rehearsal for an upcoming performance or a way of dealing with anxiety about it.

Bandages

Did you dream that you were wrapped in bandages? It may be that a part of you feels hurt and in need of healing. Look carefully at your life. Maybe there is some part that needs a little extra protection or attention.

Bank (*See also* **Money**.)

A dream of a bank refers to things that are valuable to you, and perhaps to losing them. Maybe you are just discovering something special about yourself. Dreaming of banks (or bank robbers) may be your subconscious urging you to save some money rather than spend it all.

Barefoot

Tromping through your dreams in bare feet may symbolize feeling happy and free. Or you may have removed your shoes because you are showing respect as you approach something sacred or holy. It may indicate connectedness to the earth or a feeling of being "grounded."

Basement

It may be that a fear you have buried now wants to surface. The basement may also represent your life's foundations. Are the walls solid or cracked? If you feel safe and secure in your dream basement, you may feel the same way in your life. But if your dream basement is dark, crumbling, or scary, there may be uncertainty or doubt lurking deep in your mind.

Bath

Bathing is often a ritual of cleansing and purification. Does something in your life feel dirty or soiled? This area may be ready to be washed clean. A bath is relaxing and rejuvenating, which may be just what you need if you have been stressed out lately. But if you are bathing in hot water, you may be involved in something that could get you into trouble.

Bathroom

The bathroom in your dream may be filled with people or it may be impossible to find, which is stressful and embarrassing, even in a dream. Such a dream may mean you have to relieve yourself of something (a worry or tension) but are uneasy or anxious about doing so. It may even mean you need to wake up and go!

Bean

Dreaming of growing or eating beans may deal with issues of health, nutrition, or energy. It may likewise symbolize a growing doubt or worry that needs to be resolved. Beanstalks are the climbing vine in fairy tales and may concern spiritual growth or a longing for adventure or wealth (*Jack and the Beanstalk*).

Bear

A bear can be a dangerous, stubborn, clumsy animal. Are you in a friendship with someone who is cruel or crude—or is some part of you? The dream may be alerting you to this. A dream bear may symbolize an inner need that is being neglected and may grow ferocious if not given the needed attention.

Bed

Bed is a place of security and warmth, a place of rest. This symbol may indicate a longing for peace and quiet, a need for more sleep, or concern about a close friendship that may be in trouble.

Bee

The bee symbolizes energy, creative activity, and wealth. Dreaming of bees making honey may mean that your creativity and diligence will

Bath

reap rewards; you may be involved with a positive group of friends and be growing personally. Being threatened by bees may mean that you feel pressured to conform.

Beggar

Beggars represent poverty, want, and social inferiority—and an opportunity to be charitable. Who is the beggar in the dream? It may be that a part of you feels deprived or undervalued and is struggling to survive. Do you need to ask for help? Turning away a beggar can indicate a selfish or greedy nature. Giving to a beggar may indicate the opposite.

Bell

A bell in your dreams may signal feelings of joy, harmony, and creativity. The tolling of the bell, on the other hand, may represent issues surrounding death. Bells are also common alarms. Is there something that calls for your attention?

Bicycle

The bike you are riding in a dream indicates how you are moving through life—a child's bike may mean you feel immature; a sports bike may mean you feel athletic and purposeful; a broken bike may signal fear that you won't succeed. If you are enjoying a carefree ride in your dream, it may mean that you are moving forward independently and pursuing your own path. However, if you are having trouble riding, it may mean that you are worried about your ability to get where you want to go.

Bird

Birds represent liberty, freedom, and flight. Look carefully at the type of bird in your dream (each species has its own symbolism). What the bird is doing in your dream may provide a clue to its message.

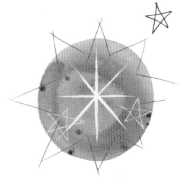

Birthday

Birthdays celebrate your life, your individuality and growth. Is yours coming up soon? Perhaps you want to feel appreciated. Gifts you receive in the dream often represent your unique talents or personal traits. A gift may also represent some aspect of the giver; it may indicate how that person has enriched your life.

Black

Pay attention to your feelings when dreaming of this color. Dreams shaded in black may indicate feelings of grief. They may also indicate something unknown or unconscious, a groping about in the dark. The color black is a symbol of mystery.

Blackboard

What is written on the blackboard? This dream may refer to a problem you are having in school or a fear of being tested in some way, in school or in your life. Or it may mean that you have mastered some new knowledge or skill.

Blindness

Things may be fuzzy and out of focus or completely dark in a dream of being blind. Either way, the dream of blindness may be calling your attention to something that is being ignored. Perhaps you are blind to the truth…or blinded by love.

Blood

Blood is a symbol of life, energy, and passion, but also of injury and disappointment. Think about the dream's action and your feelings about it. Losing blood may mean fear of losing friends or health. A blood transfusion may restore lost energy. Being "blood brothers" means having a special bond.

Blue

Blue is the color of the sea and the sky, and it often symbolizes the soul or the unconscious. Pay attention to the shade and intensity of the blue: the deeper it gets, the more it may represent sadness or depression ("feeling blue"); a light, pure blue may indicate positive thinking. The dream color may mean you are connected to nature, in need of relaxation, or merely cold.

Boat

Traveling by boat in a dream may mean adventure seeking or a passage from one phase of life to another. A boat can also represent rescue or salvation. Burning a boat means committing to something, that there is no turning back (like burning a bridge). Missing the boat means losing an opportunity.

Bomb

In dreams, bombs may symbolize violence and war or strong feelings that you are unwilling to explore. It may be a way for your unconscious to deal with feelings about these issues. Your dream may point to your own aggressive emotions or to the fact that someone is trying to control you with threats of violence. "Dropping a bomb" means delivering news that is unexpected and unpleasant.

Book

A book is a symbol of wisdom and knowledge. In a dream it may indicate a sense of satisfaction with all you have learned. The dream may be cautioning you not to focus solely on outward appearances, not to "judge a book by its cover." Being an "open book" means that your emotions and thoughts are easy for others to read.

Bread

Bread represents nourishment; in dreams, it may point to physical or spiritual needs. If you are receiving your daily bread, it may mean that you feel economically safe and secure. But if you receive only bread and water, you may feel like a prisoner.

Bridge

Bridges are symbols of transition and change, as they provide connections between places or things. A bridge provides a way across an obstacle. Perhaps you will soon find a way to overcome a fear

or problem. The bridge in your dream may also offer a way to re-establish a broken relationship. Burning bridges means that you are ending a friendship or turning your back on an opportunity.

Broom

Sweeping while you dream may relate to cleaning your internal house: you may need to get rid of some old, negative thinking and start fresh, or you may have some attitudes or behaviors that need work. It may be time to "clean up your act." What is being swept away may reveal the nature of the problem.

Brown

Brown is a symbol of earth, nature, and autumn. It may mean that you are feeling grounded. Brown can also be a sign of modesty, trustworthiness, or depression. If you are covered in brown (as in mud), it may be that you are letting others take advantage of you.

Burglar

Being burglarized in a dream may suggest that someone close to you is taking advantage of you. Look carefully at what is being stolen and from whom; the dream may point to you as the thief. Are you trying to take something that belongs to someone else? Is your own fear robbing you of some opportunity or experience?

Burn

A burn in a dream may be symbolic of anger. Is there something in your life that "burns you up?" It may be alerting you that you are being "burned" in a friendship or activity—you may be involved in something risky, something "too hot to handle."

Bus (*See also* **Car**.)

While a car is generally a symbol of the self, a bus often represents the community or involvement in a team activity or sport. Note the condition of the bus; it may indicate how you feel about what you are doing. If you dream about "missing the bus," you may regret a lost opportunity or fear that this is your last chance to get where you want to go.

Butterfly

The butterfly is a universal symbol of growth and change. If you dream of a caterpillar morphing into a butterfly, it may be that you are changing into something new or that one part of your life is ending so another can begin. Butterflies also signify grace, beauty, and freedom.

C

Cage (*See also* **Prison**.)

Did you dream you were locked in a cage? It may be that you are feeling restricted or have lost some freedom. You may be trying to lock away some part of yourself that you have difficulty accepting. But if you enter the cage of your own free will, you might desire the protection that it offers.

Calendar

A calendar in a dream may concern putting your life to good use or making the most of your time—*carpe diem* (seize the day). Or you may be getting stressed about an important project that is on the horizon. Have you been procrastinating?

Camera

The camera sees the truth; it tracks growth and changes in appearance. Perhaps you are changing in some way, but haven't noticed. Perhaps there is something you need to focus on and look at more objectively. Some primitives believe that a photograph captures the soul.

Cancer

A dream of having cancer may signal an emotional issue that is threatening you. You may be hurting yourself by keeping the emotion locked inside. If you dream that someone you love has cancer (and they are sick in real life), it may be an unconscious way of handling feelings about it.

Candle

A candle is a symbol of light overcoming darkness and may represent a quest for knowledge, wisdom, or insight. Being "a light in the world" means doing something that makes a difference. What is the mood of the dream? Candles are often lit in celebration (as on a birthday cake), as well as to set a peaceful or romantic atmosphere.

Cannon (*See also* **Weapon**.)

The cannon may deal with feelings about aggression or attack. It may be that someone or something is bombarding you mercilessly. This dream may also refer to your way of getting what you want: do you threaten others with the intense force of your personality?

Car

A car that you are driving: Car dreams generally symbolize the way you approach problems and how effectively you reach your goals. The condition and quality of the car will tell a lot about how you view yourself. Is the car sleek and sporty or a rundown old clunker? A car that is out of control may mean that you are involved in some risky behavior. A car that is difficult to start or that stalls out may be suggesting that you are having trouble moving forward or getting going.

A car that is driven by someone else: Who is driving the car? This person may represent someone in your life (or a part of your own personality) that has control over you. This dream may also tap into unresolved frustrations about not yet having your driver's license. You may feel that your freedom is limited by having to rely on others for transportation.

Cards

If you dream of playing cards, you may be treating your life as a game of chance and taking too many risks. The cards you hold may be an indication about whether or not you feel lucky. If someone else

Car

is "holding all the cards," you may feel controlled or as if something is limiting your chances to succeed.

Carnival

Carnivals offer fun and frivolity. Dreaming of one may mean that you need to lighten up and have some fun. But if you are playing the clown, you may be about to make a fool of yourself.

Castle

See **Palace**.

Cat

Cats in dreams are associated with the positive qualities of creativity, mystery, and independence and the negative qualities of cattiness, destructiveness, and territoriality. Do you—or does anyone in your life—have these cat-like traits? A cat in a dream may represent something that you fear, perhaps even some quality in yourself. Of course, a cat in a dream can also symbolize a real cat in your waking life.

Caterpillar

A caterpillar may seem gluttonous, lazy, and unattractive, but it eventually becomes a **Butterfly**. So a dream caterpillar may indicate transformation into something more beautiful or good.

Ceiling

The ceiling in a dream may represent your intellect. If you hit your head against the ceiling or it falls in on you, perhaps you have run out of ideas or are taking too narrow a view. If the ceiling is impossibly high, you may not be thinking hard enough or you may not feel smart enough to solve a problem. You may need to look at the situation from a different angle.

Cemetery

Dreaming of a cemetery likely represents **Death** or your feelings about it. Consider who in the dream has died. It may be a sign that change is needed, as it was for Scrooge in *A Christmas Carol*. Such dreams may also indicate the burying (or repressing) of emotions. Are you being buried by stress?

Chase

Being chased: The things that chase you in the night may represent your fears. You may be running from a problem you don't want to face, a person who is causing you trouble, or even a part of your own personality. Have courage. Turn around and take a look at who or what you're running from.

Chasing after something suggests there is something you want in your life. You may be feeling frustrated about achieving a goal or developing a relationship on which you are working very hard. You may feel that something or someone you care about is becoming more distant, physically or emotionally. What is it you're chasing?

Child

The child in your dreams may be a part of your personality or a symbol of your early childhood. Is the child neglected, happy, or troubled? Look for something in your own life that parallels the age or attitude of the child. The child in the dream may represent growth, energy, or future opportunities. Perhaps you miss the uncomplicated, carefree joys of childhood and are reluctant to grow up and take on more adult responsibilities.

Circle

The circle symbolizes inner unity, perfection (Jung), wholeness, and immortality. To dream of a circle may mean you are seeking completeness and excellence. Has something in your life "come full circle?" Perhaps the circle is your safe place, providing a defense against a dangerous situation or person. On the other hand, the circle may represent tedium, boredom, or frustration (as in "going around in circles") or being caught up in a "vicious circle."

Circus

See **Carnival**, **Clown**, **Acrobat**.

City

The city may symbolize your self and the different parts of your personality. It may also reflect your social environment. An important key here is what is happening in the city of your dreams. The city may represent protection or shelter in a dream, likewise progress, a loss of individuality, or a need for community. A large, bustling city may suggest over-activity, isolation, or exciting opportunities.

Cliff (*See* **Falling**.)

A cliff is a critical point; dreaming of one may indicate that you are at a time of decision. Are you ready to "take the plunge" or do you just want to give up?

Climbing

Climbing may indicate lofty goals, big dreams, or high hopes. The dream may show your determination to achieve, but it won't be easy. You will face obstacles and it will take concentration and persistence to overcome them. This dream may suggest that you are making progress.

Clock (*See also* **Time**.)

Is time running out on an important project or assignment? This dream may suggest that you are wasting time. Pay attention to the time on the clock, it may indicate your age when something important occurred or that something important is about to happen.

Clothes (*See also* **Nakedness**.)

How you are dressed in the dream can tell much about how you really feel about yourself. Clothes tattered and out-of-date? You may be feeling rundown or unattractive. Clothes don't fit? Maybe there is something in your life that isn't fitting right, either. Clothes represent the image you show the world, so in the dream they may reflect an attempt to discover your true personality. A **Uniform** or costume may symbolize a role you play in life.

Cloud

Dream clouds may indicate your emotional state: soft, fluffy clouds may represent tranquility and relaxation; storm clouds may signal frustration or depression. Light breaking through the clouds may signify a "silver lining," a positive aspect of a bad situation. If your "head is in the clouds," you may be spending too much time (or not enough) daydreaming.

Clown (*See also* **Carnival**.)

A dream of a clown may suggest concern about looking silly or making a fool of yourself; you may need to let loose and have a little fun. Are you smiling through your tears? You may be hiding your true feelings.

Color

The predominance of a color in a dream may impart special meaning. Be sure to note the intensity of the color. *See also* the individual entries for the following colors:

POSITIVE	NEGATIVE
Black: the unconscious, magic	grief, death, emotional stagnation
Blue: healing, air	emotional coldness

Brown: earth, groundedness — depression, dishonesty

Green: nature, energy, growth — jealousy, sickness

Red: love, warmth, passion — anger, violence (blood)

White: purity, innocence, peace — death, mourning, fear

Yellow: artistic inspiration — cowardliness

Compass

A compass provides orientation. It may symbolize heading in the right direction or being focused. But a spinning, directionless compass may mean that you have lost direction or are going the wrong way.

Computer

Computers enable people to do (sometimes very creative or complex) work faster and more easily. But they also eliminate a lot of social interaction. In a dream, a computer may symbolize either effective organization or robotic perfectionism. Is your focus more on things than on people? Are you devising a new application or technological advance? Or do you simply have a project due?

Cooking

Cooking transforms raw ingredients; it is a form of creative expression. It may represent personal change and development: the separate ingredients are combining into something new and wonderful.

Cow

The cow is often a maternal symbol, a source of nurturing and renewal. Mythology is filled with goddesses turning into or being aided by cows. The cow is also associated with the moon and the earth. But cows are also considered dim-witted and unattractive. What role does the cow in your dream play?

Cowboy

A dream cowboy may represent trying something new or "taming the wild frontier." It may also underscore your feelings about the freedom to be your own person.

Crying

Ever wake up crying from a dream? It may represent deep sadness, pain, or an unresolved hurt. This dream may be bringing those previously unacknowledged feelings to the surface. Perhaps it is time to examine your hurts in order to start healing them.

D

Dance

Dancing in a dream expresses energy, celebration, and transformation. Is there something new or exciting in your life? The type of dance may symbolize your feelings. Dancing with a partner often portrays the status of a friendship and your feelings about the friend. You may be rehearsing for an upcoming performance.

Darkness

Stumbling around in darkness in a dream may represent anxiety or uncertainty about the unknown or about something you don't understand. Is the dream frightening or simply frustrating? Perhaps something hidden in your unconscious needs to be brought to light. This dream may be telling you not to keep secrets that leave important grownups or parents "in the dark" about things going on in your life.

Dating

A date dream may be a way of getting to be comfortable in friendships that may involve romance or of handling anxiety about an upcoming "night out."

What happens on the date and how you feel about it are clues to your deepest feelings and thoughts about romance and dating.

Dawn

The coming of dawn, the sunrise, may be the first light of new understanding. Dawn signals fresh starts and endless possibilities. Perhaps there is a project or friendship about which you feel optimistic and hopeful. This dream may be telling you to continue and see it through.

Death

Your own death: Though it can be startling, even shocking, when you actually die in a dream, it does *not* mean that something bad is going to happen to you. The dream may instead be alerting you to self-destructive behavior or an unhealthy friendship. Death dreams may point to an area in your life that is going wrong or is undergoing major change.

The death of someone you know: This dream may tempt you to warn the person, but again, it does *not* mean something bad is going to happen. It may be that the person who dies is someone important to you but whom you are neglecting or treating badly. If so, it may signal that the friend-

✳ Dating ✳

ship is in trouble. Perhaps the dead person represents a part of your personality, say a talent that you aren't using. The dream may refer to feelings of abandonment or insecurity.

Debt

Have you broken a promise or failed to live up to someone's standards? This dream may be the result: it may signify guilt or a debt, burden, or obligation. Perhaps you need to work on a friendship or say you're sorry.

This dream may also reflect an unbalanced attitude toward money and thrift. You may be spending too much time, energy, or money on "things." Have you spent your resources badly on a project or friendship that is not well thought out? Do you feel too much responsibility toward someone?

Deer (See also **Antelope**.)

The deer symbolizes personal freedom. It may symbolize shyness or an escape to solitude.

Deformity

See **Abnormal/Abnormality**.

Desert

Wandering through the desert in a dream may symbolize feeling emotionally isolated, drained, lonely, or hopeless. Do you feel out of sync with friends or family? Perhaps you need to reconnect and have some fun. Alternatively, the desert may be a place of spiritual renewal or testing. This may be a time when facing problems will lead to new insight and growth.

Detective

Detective dreams often point to a search for your unique qualities and talents, your hidden truths. What are you searching for? Is there some "mystery" you'd like to unravel? These dreams may also suggest adventure and excitement.

Diamond

A diamond is a symbol of light and brilliance, purity and wholeness. In a dream, it may represent something rare and beautiful in you, perhaps moral or intellectual wisdom that gives you character and strength. If you are hoarding diamonds in your dream, it may reflect vanity or greed.

Dictator

Dictators have absolute authority. Is there anyone in your life like this? You may feel that someone is controlling you and wish for more freedom and authority. Explore what happens and how you feel about the dictator in this dream. Is it possible that you're the dictator?

Dinosaur

Dinosaurs are huge, majestic, and extinct. Perhaps their sheer size fascinates you. But as something extraordinary that is lost, they may be pointing you toward some important memory or goal that you have put aside. Their size and power may refer to the authority or importance of parental figures.

Dirt

Is there a part of your life that feels dirty? Have you done something that you feel is wrong? This dream may be readying you to be cleansed (*see* **Bath**) or to clean up a problem.

Disability

A dream of an emotional or mental handicap may concern a weakness or need in your life. Perhaps you aren't using all of your abilities. The flip side is that it may express arrogance or exaggerated importance. You may need to show more compassion to others or be more responsible or helpful.

Do you feel as if you have lost your freedom or that some part of your life or personality is being held back? Perhaps you feel stuck or unable to move toward a goal;

you may doubt yourself or feel inferior. You may be in need of help if you are asking too much of yourself. Are there people in your life who could provide the needed support?

Disguise (*See also* **Mask**, **Uniform**, **Wig**.)

In a dream, disguises may symbolize trying out a different personality, taking on a new role, or developing a hidden talent or ability. Wearing a disguise may mask feelings of inferiority; it suggests hiding from the truth or trying to give a false impression. A disguise that imitates the look of someone else may hint at a desire to be like that person in some way.

Diving (*See* also **Air**.)

Diving is similar to **Flying**; it often represents freedom and adventure, or readiness to take a risk ("to take the plunge"). It may mean that you are ready to delve deep into your hidden potential. Perhaps you plan to "dive right in" to some project or friendship. If you swim or dive in real life, this dream may be unconscious practice for an upcoming meet.

Divorce

Divorce in a dream may point to feelings about separation. You may be feeling that an important friendship is in danger or grieving a marriage that is dissolving. In some cases, dreaming of divorce indicates your growing separateness from your parents and your increasing ability to make independent judgments and decisions.

Doctor

Doctors in dreams are often similar to the **Wise Old Man/Wise Old Woman**. They offer wisdom and guidance. The doctor in your dream may be pointing to an area of your life that is sick or has been neglected and is in need of healing attention. Listen carefully to what the doctor tells you—it may be your unconscious providing clues to healing yourself. If you are the doctor, this dream may refer to your role as a helper. Is your help needed or are you getting in the way of recovery?

Dog

The dog in your dream may be a companion, a guide, or an attacker. It may represent a friend or a part of your personality. Dreaming about a loving, faithful dog may mean you are confident about your friends and are loyal to them; it may also indicate loyalty to yourself, especially to your core values.

A pack of dogs on the attack may indicate concern about following the crowd in doing something that may be wrong or dangerous.

Doll (*See also* **Puppet**, **Teddy Bear**.)

The doll in your dream may offer comfort, unconditional love, or a return to the simplicity of childhood. These qualities may be particularly attractive right now. The doll may symbolize vulnerability or fragility (a "china doll"). Are you too easily hurt? Are you being treated like a pretty object, with your thoughts and feelings not being taken into account?

Dolphin

The dolphin is a wise, inquisitive mammal with a reputation for helping sailors and swimmers and for warning them of danger; it is often a symbol of salvation, as is the **Anchor**. A swim with dolphins refers to freedom, wholeness, and connection with nature. Dolphins may bring thoughts and wishes from the unconscious to the surface.

Donkey

Donkeys are often viewed as stupid and stubborn, but this stubbornness can be a good thing when the donkey does what is right and goes his own way against the crowd.

Donkeys are hardworking and humble; they are the beasts upon which kings and prophets often rode. Is the donkey in your dream carrying someone special? If you are leading the donkey, it depicts your leadership and persuasiveness.

Door

An open door may indicate a new opportunity or phase of life; it may be a portal to change, growth, or transformation. Open doors also offer shelter and protection from the storms of life. A closed door may represent an obstacle, a lost opportunity, or something unknown or scary. You may need to open the door to see what is behind it.

Dove

The dove is a symbol of peace and purity, and dreaming of one may indicate reconciliation and friendship. The dove is also a spiritual symbol; as such, it may offer divine inspiration or spiritual guidance.

Dragon

A dragon (or snake) is often seen as the opposite of a **Dove**. Aggressive and dangerous, a dragon is the evil standing in the way of (or guarding) something good; you may have to slay the dragon to reach your goal. In Chinese tradition, dragons represent imperial power and bring good luck.

Driver's License (*See also* **Car**.)

Getting your driver's license is a rite of passage into adulthood. This dream may anticipate the day when you are given the privilege to drive. It may refer to increasing responsibility or achieving a clearer identity. Losing your driver's license may represent a loss of freedom, identity, or maturity. Searching for your driver's license may represent your own search for individual identity.

Drowning

Many see drowning as symbolic of being overwhelmed by the subconscious or of being flooded with emotion. Do you have hidden thoughts or feelings that threaten to break free? This dream may also represent a lack of planning that now swamps you with work or stress.

Drum

The drum is an ancient means of communication. Is there something you need to tell someone? Drums are used as a call for help and a call to war. A drumbeat can imitate the heart rhythm. Dreaming of drums may indicate that you are alarmed or in need of help.

Drum

E

Eagle
The eagle can fly higher and faster, and see farther, than any other creature; thus, it stands for freedom, strength, and clarity of vision. The eagle also represents patriotism, sovereignty, and power.

Ear
The ear is the organ of hearing. It may be that you need to pay more attention—you may be missing something important. The dream may be encouragement to listen to your inner voice; alternatively, you may be listening to the wrong things. Have you been hearing or spreading gossip?

Earth
Earth is home and the source and foundation for all of life. As such, it is a symbol of mother—protection, nurture, and nourishment. It may symbolize respect for nature, home, or family. The dream may suggest feeling grounded or connected to the energy derived from earth.

Earthquake
In dreams, an earthquake may be a symbol of sudden change, emotional upset, or self-destructive energy. An earthquake may rock your belief system and shatter your strongly held convictions (Jung). Perhaps your foundation is shaky. It may be necessary to modify your point of view and rebuild on solid ground.

Echo
Are you repeating yourself? You may feel that no one is listening to you, that you are being ignored. Alternatively, the echo may be a repetition of something important that you have not attended to. Consider what is being said.

Egg
The egg is a symbol of beginning, resurrection, and regeneration. Is there something new in your life or that needs renewal? Eggs represent potential and possibility, but they are very fragile. You may be optimistic about your goals and plans, but they need care and protection. Be careful not to put all your eggs into one basket.

Electricity
Electricity is energy. In a dream, it may signal that you're operating at full power. Are the power lines down? Your energy may be running low. Electrical sparks may point to inner tension or imbalance.

Elephant

Elephants may represent the power of the unconscious: like the elephant of proverbs, the unconscious has a prodigious memory, it never forgets. A dream of an elephant may be an offering of the wisdom and force that the unconscious contains. Elephants are thick-skinned; they may be urging you to be more patient and tactful, and not to take criticism so seriously.

Elevator

An elevator symbolizes emotional change. Going up quickly points to high hopes and worthy aspirations. Going down? This may suggest fear of failure or feelings of inferiority. An elevator that gets stuck may signify a lack of direction or goals.

Elf

Elves are mythical beings that often possess magical powers. In your dreams they may serve as guides to the soul (Jung) or to greater understanding of your unconscious life. They may also represent a more mystical, natural, or fairy-tale kind of existence.

Embarrassment

Embarrassing yourself in a dream is a way of exposing your imperfections and freeing yourself from the need to be perfect. You may need to let go of some self-imposed restrictions and limitations. Don't be afraid to laugh at yourself every now and then. This dream may also point out areas where you feel vulnerable or insecure.

Engagement

See **Marriage**, **Wedding**.

Entanglement

Are you ensnared, bound, or trapped by an obstacle? This dream may be urging you to take charge, rid yourself of restraints, and impose order. Note what it is that binds you—a friendship, an idea. Another possibility is that you feel overwhelmed or restricted by obligations. Do you have goals that are not being met because of other burdens in your life?

Escape (*See also* **Chase**.)

What you are trying to escape is an important key to understanding this dream. Very often you are trying to avoid a part of yourself that needs to be explored: it may be a scary situation or a friendship with which you feel unable to cope. In escaping, you are getting to some better place.

Escape

Exam

Failing an exam or realizing you must soon take an exam for which you are unprepared is a common theme in dreams. The dream may have you about to take a final when you haven't attended the class all year, you have overslept, or you can't find the classroom and are going to be late. You may even be onstage and unable to remember your lines. This dream often reflects anxiety about an upcoming project or event; you may be feeling frustrated, insecure, or in over your head. If you're taking the test with confidence or getting good grades in the dream, enjoy it. You feel sure of yourself and in control.

Excavation

This dream may suggest that some important work needs to be done in your life; it may involve some hidden potential or repressed emotion that is deeply buried. What is being uncovered? What are your feelings about it and about the work being done? Whatever labor or rearranging of your thoughts and beliefs is involved may be well worth the effort. You may be digging for buried treasure.

Extraterrestrial

This dream figure may represent an unknown part of your self, something hidden or unexplored, possibly qualities or goals yet to be discovered. Does any part of you feel as if it's "from outer space"? This dream may deal with accepting that part. You may be feeling alienated—different from and unconnected to friends and family. Are you longing for close personal connection? This dream may signify adventure or exploration of the unknown and mysterious.

Eye

The eye being considered the window to the soul, this dream may be pointing toward greater awareness or understanding of your self. Looking yourself in the eye means seeing yourself honestly. The dream may concern something it's important for you to see: you may have missed it earlier or be afraid that you will miss it.

Eyeglasses

As a dream symbol, eyeglasses may help put your life into focus. Perhaps your vision or your point of view is slightly fuzzy. You might want to take a closer look at something. Conversely, the glasses may keep you from seeing clearly. Do the glasses belong to someone else? You may need to focus on your own point of view. If the glasses are rose-colored, you may be seeing life unrealistically. Of course, if you wear glasses, this dream may deal with concerns about your appearance.

F

Face

Your face is what you show the world. It represents your identity and your feelings about yourself. The expression may identify your underlying emotions. You may be wearing a **Mask** when you want to hide your inner feelings. Having two faces shows a deceptive nature. A blank expression may mean you are unwilling to face up to something or that there is something you need to confront.

Factory

What is the atmosphere in the factory? If negative, your life may have become monotonous, an unchanging routine; you may feel isolated or that you are losing individuality. A positive factory environment may reflect your involvement in a worthwhile community project or team effort.

Your different psychological parts may be working well together.

Fairy

See **Elf**.

Fairy Godmother

A fairy godmother in a dream may represent help in overcoming difficulties, as in *Cinderella*. You may lack confidence in your abilities and wish for a magical escape from your problems.

Falling

Falling dreams are among the most common types; the dreamer often awakes in fear. The dream may underscore some anxiety in your life, such as failing at something or being put down by someone you want to impress. Falling dreams may signal that your life feels out of control. You may be overwhelmed trying to keep it all together or anxious about letting go. Falling dreams may hint at arrogant or self-destructive behavior.

Family

Dreaming about family (or a group that appears in your dream to be your family) may represent your need for connection, security, or love. How do you feel about your family? It is often possible in dreams to work through issues with family, to deal with anger, resentment, love, and betrayal. Sometimes these issues are too emotional to face in daily life. The family in dreams may also represent different parts of your personality that are coming together.

Famous People

Did a celebrity show up in your dream? How exciting! What is the famous person doing in your dream? Do you like him or her? If something about the celebrity reminds you of yourself or of someone else in your life, the figure may represent an attitude or characteristic of yours or of someone close to you. If the star doesn't remind you of anyone and is flattering you with a lot of attention, perhaps you need a boost in your self-esteem.

Farm/Farmer

Farming is associated with growth, productivity, and nourishment, and the farmer is often seen as the agent that manages the cycles of growth, harvest, and renewal. A farm or farmer in a dream may represent the fulfilling of basic needs or sustenance. It may also represent your ability to produce. Given that you reap what you sow,

consider what it is you're planting. Is it something good or not? Is your farm thriving or neglected?

Father

If you dream of your father, you may be trying to work through issues in your relationship with your dad. As with **Family**, you may be trying to work out ambivalent feelings of love, frustration, and anger while you sleep. Fathers often represent authority and striving for achievement. Because of the father's association with authority and morality, dreaming of your father may indicate a guilty conscience. The father may also represent your feelings about other authority figures. According to C.G. Jung, the father represents the intellect and the collective unconscious.

Fear

The fears that appear in dreams often mirror waking fears and insecurities. What is it that frightened you? It may have been a real-life event. Does life feel out of control? You may be afraid of failing or concerned with what others think of you. Keep in mind that anger and fear are closely related and even the strength itself of your own feelings can be scary. Pay attention to the ending of the dream. It may provide an answer about how to overcome your fears.

Feather

You may dream of being "light as a feather," feeling free and unencumbered, with nothing to weigh you down. Or it may be that your thoughts are scattered (making you "feather-brained").

Fence

Fences in dreams often represent barriers you have erected as protection from real or imagined fears. What is the fence meant to keep out? Does it bring isolation and restriction or a sense of security? Does the fence perhaps symbolize some social boundary imposed on you: rules or inhibitions? It may also represent an obstacle or a decision you're putting off ("sitting on the fence").

Fever

In real life, fever is a warning; it's a symptom of illness. Look carefully at yourself and your friendships—something may be sick. Fevers also represent restlessness and delusions. Are you being deceived?

Fight (*See also* **Quarrel**.)

Fighting in a dream expresses conflict, either within your self or with others. Are you wrestling with a problem? Are you in an argumentative friendship? This dream may be helping you deal with your aggression and anger. You may also be battling inconsistencies in your beliefs and actions, struggling to make up your mind.

Finger

The pointing finger in your dream may be offering you direction. But pointing is also considered rude and ill mannered. Is it a finger of blame pointing at you? Most often, this blame is self-imposed. Cutting off your fingers in a dream indicates that you are in mourning or that you are a thief. "Sticky fingers" also refers to thievery. Crossing fingers is a wish for luck. If you are "all thumbs," it means that you feel awkward.

Fire

A well-tended fire is a source of light, heat, and energy and may represent your passion for life. It is often necessary to "go through the fire" metaphorically in order to be cleansed and made whole, so dreaming of fire also represents purification or transformation. When allowed to get free, fire can be wildly destructive. Have your feelings gotten out of control?

Flea

If you dream of these itchy para-sites, you or someone in your life may be acting petty or being a pest. You may be feeling jumpy. Does the dream make you feel in need of a **Bath** or a good **Cleaning**? Perhaps the flea represents some-thing that makes you feel dirty.

Flood (*See also* **Drowning**, **Swimming**.)

Water in dreams often represents the unconscious, and dreams of flooding can be caused by being emotionally overwhelmed. Your feelings threaten to sweep you away. Try to identify these feelings and find a way to express them, to be more comfortable with them. Though it can be destructive, flood-water also fertilizes, making for new growth. You may need to relax and learn to swim with your emotions.

Floor

The floor often represents the basic, ground level foundation of your life. Its condition may be a key to your attitude about yourself and your life. Falling to the floor may suggest you reevaluate your core values. Are you on solid ground?

Flower

In dreams, flowers often under-score love and friendship. Flowers

Fish/Fisherman/Fishing

Lakes and seas are representative of the unconscious. Fish are often symbolic of emotions and ancient beliefs deep in the unconscious; fishing means bringing these to the surface. Dreaming of fish may also mean that you feel comfortable in your environment ("swimming like a fish") or—if the fish is beached—out of your element ("like a fish out of water").

Flag

A flag is a symbol of national identi-fication and patriotism. Flags flying in your dream may represent a love of your homeland. Flags or banners also symbolize both war and victory. A white flag means surrender; a black flag symbolizes criminals or pirates; a red flag is a warning of danger; and a yellow flag is a sign of illness. A flag at half-mast symbolizes mourning.

convey sympathy and symbolize beauty, attraction, and romance. Flowers also symbolize the brevity of life—the perfection of their bloom lasts only days. Do you have concerns about the shortness of life or the length of a friendship?

Flying

Flying dreams are quite common. They are generally fun and enjoyable—even breathtaking. It is important to note how you feel about flying in the dream. Flying can represent freedom and joy in movement, the achieving of lofty dreams and goals, or feelings of competence or success. But flying may also be a way to show off; in this case, you may feel stressed and anxious about your ability to perform. Dreams in which you try to fly but can't get off the ground may point to some obstacle that prevents you from being successful.

Fog

Fog represents a lack of understanding or confusion about what to do or where to go. You may be puzzled about something and need to have it explained more clearly. It may also be that your life lacks focus or direction.

Food

Being so basic to existence, food appears often in dreams. It is important to note the qualities of the dream food—delicious or bland, nutritious or unhealthy— and how you feel about the food you are eating. Different foods have different meanings for individual dreamers. Food dreams may point to something that is lacking or a need for energy or strength. Perhaps some part of you feels malnourished or unhealthy. On the other hand, food may represent a special treat or a source of comfort. What you are eating in the dream may provide a clue to what you need in your life.

If there is not enough food, you may doubt that you have what it takes to succeed or you may not trust what you have. If you eat too much or too little in your dream, you may have issues with your weight or your body.

Fool

See **Clown**.

Foot

The foot may symbolize independence, the ability to make your own way or find your own path. It may represent your individual foundation: your principles and values. Your feet

Flying

indicate the direction in which you are headed. If you trample someone or something underfoot, you may be taking advantage of someone or treating him or her badly. If you always land on your feet, you feel lucky in life. Having two left feet means that you feel awkward.

Forest

The forest is wild—uncontrolled and uncultivated. In dreams, it often represents the unconscious and the instinctive drives and emotions that reside there. Is the forest dark and threatening? It may conceal urges or secrets you prefer not to know. You may be so focused on one aspect of a thing that you can't "see the forest for the trees." The forest may be a symbol for your youth and inexperience ("like a babe in the woods") or for an uncomfortable situation in which you feel stuck ("you're not out of the woods yet").

Fork

A fork may appear in a **Food** dream. It may represent spiteful-ness in a friendship. Do you or does someone you know speak with a "forked tongue"? A fork in the road may indicate an impor-tant decision about your future.

Four (*See also* **Numbers**.)

According to C.G. Jung, the number four represents personal growth and wholeness. It may be that you are on your way to becoming complete. In a dream, the number may also symbolize order, uniformity, and stability. It represents the four seasons, the four directions on a compass, and the four elements (water, air, earth, and fire). It may also indicate your age (or the time) when something important happened.

Fox

The fox is cunning, wily, sneaky ("sly as a fox"), and a trickster ("crazy like a fox") and flatterer. It is also clever and smart. Do you know anyone with these traits? Do you have any of them yourself?

Friend

Pay attention to the characteristics of the friend in the dream. Are they familiar? Friends in dreams whom you haven't seen in a long time in waking life probably represent certain qualities of personality or behavior in you or in others: they don't usually point to the actual person. People appearing in dreams who are close to you in real life may also represent qualities in yourself, but more often they refer to your relationship with that person. What does the dream tell you? You may want to look at how you really feel about your relationship.

Frog

Because they are amphibious (they can live on land or in the water), frogs in dreams may mean that you feel ambivalent about something, that you have feelings both positive and negative. If you view frogs with disgust, there may be something in your life that you feel is equally disgusting. But, as in *The Frog Prince*, a frog can represent inner beauty, as well as transformation from a thing you loathe into something wonderful.

Frozen

See **Ice**.

Fruit

Fruit is often a symbol of ripeness, abundance, and life. Ripe and delicious fruit may mean you feel good about your life and your activities; your efforts will "bear fruit." Rotten fruit may point to feelings of inferiority, illness, or wasted opportunity. Picking fresh fruit is encouragement to "seize the day." Dreaming of fruit may also be your body's way of telling you to eat more healthy food.

Funeral

Do you have a bad habit or a destructive way of thinking or feeling that needs to "die"? The funeral dream may be alerting you to this unhealthy tendency. If the funeral deals with a friendship, that friendship may be in danger. Perhaps it is time to bury your differences. A funeral dream may also be part of the grieving process if someone close to you has died.

G

Gag

If your mouth is gagged in this obstacle dream, you may feel restricted in what you are allowed to say or unable to express a need. Is there an area in your life about which you have to keep quiet? It may also signal that you are talking too much or telling the secrets of others.

Game

Pay attention to the game you are playing. This dream could be a suggestion to have more fun, not to take things so seriously. If you're winning, you may feel good about your life. If you're losing, you may be unsure about your ability to succeed. What are the rules of the game? They may indicate your values and attitudes about life. Are you playing fair or are you cheating?

Garbage

If you dream about garbage, it may be time to clean up some of the worries, burdens, or fears that are bringing you down. Emotional garbage accumulates unless you discard it regularly. As you sift through your internal trash, you may find buried treasure—valuable insights or unsuspected talents and abilities. This dream could also stem from concerns about nature and preserving the environment.

Garden

Beautiful things often grow in a garden; it symbolizes balance, growth, and relaxation. The garden is cultivated and cared for, unlike the **Forest**, so it often represents the consciousness and the "civilized" (acceptable) thoughts and feelings. Perhaps, at least on a conscious level, your life is well ordered and peaceful. A blooming garden means that you have talents and possibilities that are developing; you are ready for personal and spiritual growth. If you seek sanctuary in a garden, you may need protection from the difficulties of everyday life.

Gasoline

Are you running out of gas? It may be that your energy is running low. You may need to take a break or find a way to regain your strength.

Gate (*See also* **Door**.)

A gate provides passage, and so is a symbol of transition. What is on the other side? An open gate represents welcome and friendship. A closed gate may indicate rejection. In any case, a gate leads toward change and growth.

Ghost

This dream may suggest you are chasing something that doesn't exist; check that your thoughts and ideas aren't simply illusions. You may need to change your way of thinking or put aside something from your past that continues to haunt you. Ghosts may also be expressions of a guilty conscience.

Garden

Giant

A giant may symbolize adulthood and the long process of change and growth that lead there. The giant in your dream could thus be a frightening figure or one who brings good news, depending on how you feel about growing up. Giants may represent authority—those who command, protect, and punish. What is the role of the giant in your dream? Giant dreams may also indicate big possibilities that are coming your way. Alternatively, they may hint at a problem that is too big to handle.

Gift (*See also* **Birthday**.)

Pay attention to the gift that is given or received. Gifts often symbolize the relationship with the giver. Is it something desirable, something to be cherished? Then the dream may be telling you about the value of the friendship. If it is something unpleasant, then consider your feelings about the giver. This dream may also be encouragement to share your joy and your life with others.

Giraffe

Are you "sticking your neck out"? You may be taking an important stand or entertaining lofty thoughts. This dream may also concern seeking a different perspective, a higher view.

Girl (*See also* **Child**.)

Dreaming of a little girl may represent lightheartedness and innocence. Pay attention to the girl in the dream and her general mood and behavior. That may be a clue as to how you feel about your self or your feminine qualities.

Glass

Glass has a beautiful transparent quality. It may represent purity and spirituality. Because it is so delicate, it is also a symbol of fragility and short-lived beauty. Broken glass may indicate feelings of injury or a loss of innocence. If you live in a glass house in your dream, you may be feeling vulnerable or exposed.

Glove

This dream may be telling you that something or someone is exactly right—it fits perfectly, "like a glove." However, gloves may also symbolize protection. Perhaps you feel the need to defend yourself or to fight for your rights. Gloves prevent direct contact. Are you detached from others? Maybe something in your life feels dirty or prickly. White gloves represent cleanliness.

Gold

Because of its beauty and worth, gold may represent those qualities in you, your most prized possessions. Gold is the most sought-after metal, but it is also the most elusive. Immune to tarnish, gold symbolizes spiritual riches and enduring value; it is viewed as incorruptible. Is there anything in your life that has or needs this kind of unchanging beauty? Gold also represents the sun, the source of light and warmth.

Goodbye

It may be time to let go of something if you say goodbye to it in a dream. Pay attention to what or whom you are leaving. Does the parting bring relief or is it sad? You may be facing changes in your life or taking on new responsibilities. Do you need to let go of immature or childish behavior?

Goose

Are you afraid of acting foolish or stupid, of being a "silly goose"? In dreams, that same goose may be a symbol of love and sacrifice. The goose that lays the golden egg produces something precious and wonderful; it may be the treasure you are seeking. But if you kill the goose to get the golden eggs inside, you may be acting thoughtlessly and greedily.

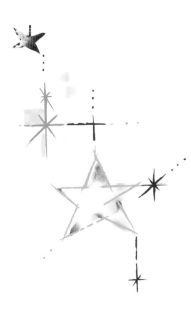

Grain

Grain often symbolizes intellectual and personal needs. Are you being productive? If the harvest is bountiful, then you are filled with self-confidence and vitality. If the crop is poor or damaged, you may feel inferior or weak.

Grass

Grass represents quick growth, a sense of being grounded and useful. If the grass is fresh and green you may be feeling healthy and connected to nature; if the grass is withered or burnt you may be discouraged or depressed. If the grass is growing wild, perhaps you are being unreasonable or seeking greater freedom; if the grass has just been cut, you may be conforming or following conventional wisdom.

Gray

The color gray in your dreams may signal that you are not sure about something; it may not be clear. The dream may be pushing you to make a clear distinction between right and wrong. Alternatively, the color may represent the unconscious or the gray fog of depression.

Green

Green is the color of growth; it may signal personal development and maturity or health and fertility. But a putrid green may indicate illness—something may be rotten. Green is also the color of jealousy and poison. Pay attention to the shade of green and the feeling it evokes.

Greenhouse (*See also* **Glass**.)

Are you judging others too harshly, even though you have problems of your own? You may be hiding your anger for fear of breaking something or hurting someone by expressing it. On the other hand, this dream may be telling you to be more open and transparent. A greenhouse is a place where things grow; are you working toward an important goal?

Gypsy

The gypsy may represent adventure, travel, clairvoyance (fortune telling), or intuition. The gypsy is also a symbolic scapegoat—someone who is persecuted or wrongly blamed for something. Is there a situation like this in your life?

H

Hair (*See also* **Baldness**.)

Traditionally, hair symbolizes strength, energy, and spiritual force. A full head of hair represents freedom, success, and protection from evil. The loss of hair, either by cutting or by its falling out, may represent a failure or a loss of power or self-esteem. Cutting hair may also be a symbol

Hair

of mourning. Hair dreams may point to intellectual and spiritual development; increasing vitality or freedom; or concern about your appearance. Are you thinking about a hair appointment?

Hallway

A hallway represents direction and restriction; it provides access to all the rooms within a structure, but it is up to you what doors you open. Are you facing a decision? The hallway may be a symbol of confinement in a narrow space. If you are unable to reach the end of a long hallway, you may be feeling frustrated or stuck in some area of your life. What is your goal or destination?

Halo

Does a halo encircle someone in your dream? You may believe he or she has special intellectual or spiritual ability or hold the person in great esteem. Examine whether he or she deserves to be on a pedestal.

Hammer

The hammer is a symbol of power. It can be used constructively to build and destructively to beat or tear down. It may be that you are wielding your power too forcefully and causing destruction in a friendship or situation. But you may also be building a concept or hammering together a project.

Hand

The hand in dreams often represents strength and ability: to do work; to express yourself; to reach out and take action. If the hands are withered or weak you may feel unqualified or unable to succeed at your work. Hands represent protection; hands joined together represent peace and friendship. A raised hand symbolizes an unbreakable promise. A hand over your heart means love or patriotism.

Harbor

The harbor represents a safe haven from the storms of life, a place of security when you feel threatened. Perhaps you need help coping with something difficult. However, the harbor is also a starting point for adventure. It is where you ready your confidence and prepare for the journey ahead.

Harvest (*See also* **Grain.**)

Dreams of bringing in the harvest may represent accomplishing your goals. What is it that you want to achieve? An abundant harvest may mean that you feel confident and successful. A poor or withered harvest may represent failure or feelings of inferiority.

Hat

Hats in dreams often point to your intelligence, your thoughts, and your beliefs. What is under the hat? The dream may indicate intellectual snobbery (you consider yourself better than everyone else) or repression (you hide what you are thinking and feeling). Changing hats represents changing your mind.

Head

The head represents insight, intelligence, and reason. Being fuzzy-headed may mean that you aren't thinking clearly. If you "lose your head," you may be acting without thinking. The head may also be a source of wisdom and spiritual direction, so pay attention to its message.

Heart

The heart is the seat of the emotions, representing love and affection as well as suffering. The head may be the source of reason, but what the heart tells you is no less important. In fact, it may offer greater truth. Do you have a broken heart? Perhaps you are in anguish over a lost friendship. If you are doing something with your whole heart, then you are committed to it. A good heart means that you have compassion for others and a strong heart means courage and vitality.

Heaven

Heaven is where things of the spirit are thought to reside, so dreams of heaven may represent spiritual understanding or growth. Heavenly dreams may also represent something wonderful in your life, something hopeful and optimistic. The qualities and structure of the heaven you dream about may characterize you as well.

Heel

The heel may represent your most vulnerable point, as in "Achilles' heel." Are you too focused on your weakness? The dream may also deal with being grounded (having a firm emotional, intellectual, or spiritual foundation) or with "healing" in some area of your life.

Height

In this dream you may be striving for success or hoping to grow in your abilities. You may be going through a real physical growth spurt. This dream may also be a caution against arrogance—are you trying to tower over others?

Helmet (*See also* **Hat**.)

A helmet protects your head. Perhaps you have thoughts or beliefs that you feel you must defend. But the helmet is also a symbol of invisibility—do you have thoughts you don't want anyone else to know about?

Help, inability to call for

This distressing dream may depict you in a confusing, dangerous, or scary situation where, for some reason, you can't get anyone's help or attention. What is it in the dream that prompts your distress; it may parallel a situation in your waking life. You may feel powerless or trapped, or unable to confront a problem—you may even be unaware of the danger. This dream may be urging you to seek help.

Hermit

A hermit is someone who has abandoned life among people, often to seek spiritual insight. You may want to be alone, to escape a frustrating social situation, or to protect yourself from intrusion. You may feel that your energy is depleted and you need to restore your inner resources. Or it may be the contrary; you may feel isolated and want more social contact.

A hermit is generally seen as trustworthy and often as a sign-post, showing the way through trouble or darkness. The dream hermit may be seeking to impart some wisdom.

Hero/Heroine (*See also* **Journey**, **Knight**.)

A dream of a hero or heroine brings your essential strengths and weaknesses of character into focus—self-knowledge that is crucial to healthy psychological development. This dream figure may symbolize being admired or validated, or such virtues as strength, courage, and nobility. On the other hand, it may be that you want someone to come and take away all of your problems.

Highway (*See also* **Car**.)

The highway may represent your feelings about your **Journey** through life. If you are moving along quickly and easily, you may feel in charge of your life and confident of your direction. If you are stuck in traffic or having trouble getting on the road, you may feel inadequate, stranded, or not up to the challenge. Accidents, breakdowns, or flat tires on the highway often correspond to problems in your waking life.

Hole

Crawling through a hole may represent passage to a different place or an approach to "wholeness." Holes are often viewed as mythical places of transformation—something may be about to change. Falling into a hole may represent failure or feelings of insecurity; being in a hole may indicate depression. A hole may also symbolize a flaw in your thinking or something in your personality that is incomplete or unseen.

Home

See **House**.

Honey

Eating honey in your dreams may indicate satisfaction in an accomplishment. Honey represents affection, pleasure, riches, and luxury—in short, the sweetness of life. If someone speaks to you in words like honey, they may be trying to trick you with flattery.

Horse

Horses represent vitality, energy, and the power of the instinct. Wild horses symbolize unbridled freedom and pure physical force. Riding a horse may signify control of your natural instincts and the directing of your power to positive ends.

Hospital

If you dream of a hospital stay, it may be that you need help with an emotional issue. The "illness" or problem that put you in the hospital may give clues to that issue. You may simply need a break, time to recover and heal. An **Operation** may point to an unhealthy attitude or a bad habit that needs removal. The dream may also refer to anxiety about your health or that of someone close to you.

Hotel

A hotel may symbolize a rest stop on the journey through life, a temporary shelter. You may be going through a change and need a little break. Perhaps you are in transition between two phases of life. Hotels also represent relaxation and adventure (a vacation).

House

A house may represent security, love, and warmth. Since it can also be a symbol for the self, be sure to note the condition of the house and how you feel being there. You may dream of places where you used to live. What was happening when you lived there? Your dream may point to a similar situation now. New rooms discovered in a familiar house may symbolize your

Horse

emerging qualities or talents. A dream of someone else's home may refer to that person's characteristics. How does that person figure in your life?

Hunger

Some area of your life is being neglected or is unfulfilled. You may need physical, emotional, or spiritual nourishment. Alternatively, this dream may be your body's way of telling you to get up and fix a midnight snack.

J

Ice

In dreams, ice may symbolize emotional coldness or distance, or unyielding attitudes; someone or something in your life may feel rigid and immobile. If you are emotionally "iced up," you may be unable to release your potential. Warming things up a bit may give you access to great possibilities. A dream of falling through the ice may signal a dangerous or precarious situation ("thin ice").

Ice Cream (*See also* **Food**.)

Ice cream often represents the pleasures of summer—its warmth and sunshine—or a special treat. Perhaps you need to treat yourself to something nice. Melting ice cream may symbolize disappointment.

Illness

Are you sick in your dream? Consider the kind of illness and how you feel when you awaken. This dream can provide valuable information about your health— physical, emotional, or mental. Your body may be signaling an oncoming disease or cautioning you to take better care of yourself.

Injury

Consider where your body is injured and how it happened. This dream may deal with some hurt you have experienced or with which you are being threatened; you may feel vulnerable or under attack. It may refer to an old injury that needs to heal. Have you hurt someone else?

Insect

Dream insects symbolize cooperative and instinctive behavior. What insects do you see in your dream? If they fascinate you, the insects in your dream may represent the positive qualities you associate with them. But if you have a "yuck!" response, they probably represent your conflict or disgust with annoying people or situations in your life.

Invisibility

If you dream of being invisible, you may be feeling rejected, ignored, or neglected. You may be ignoring an emotion or problem, hoping it will disappear. Could you be failing to recognize one of your own valuable inner resources? Then again, perhaps you are trying to accomplish an important goal without attracting attention. Invisibility can make for all kinds of supernatural adventures—you may be dreaming of Harry Potter.

Invitation

Did you receive a longed-for invitation in your dream? You may want acceptance or popularity. If the invitation doesn't come, you may be feeling rejected. In any case, loneliness and isolation are the theme. Try giving yourself permission to join the party.

Iron/Ironing

Iron represents stability, durability, and determination. This dream may be encouragement to stay strong. Tools and weapons can be made of iron; you may be acting harshly or being inflexible. Is the iron rusty? It may need a bit of cleaning.

If you dream about ironing, something in your life may need to be straightened out or smoothed over. What are you ironing?

Island

If the island is deserted and desolate, you may be feeling isolated or lonely, cut off from friends and family; conversely, you may want respite from other people. If the island is lush and beautiful, perhaps it is a place of relaxation or refuge. It may suggest a tropical adventure.

J

Jacket (*See also* **Clothing**.)

The jacket may represent the image you project to those around you. Is it stylish, shabby? The condition of the jacket may hint at your feelings about this image. Perhaps you are simply a little cold and need to warm up a bit.

Jail (*See also* **Cage**, **Prison**.)

Have you lost some freedom? A situation or relationship may have you feeling stuck. You may feel restricted or confined. Or this dream may concern guilt for a recent wrongdoing.

Island

Jam/Jelly

People in fear are sometimes said to "quiver like jelly" and the stuff can signify an unpleasant situation, as in being "in a jam." But jam is sweet, so it may symbolize a pleasant thing as well.

Jewelry (*See also* **Diamond**.)

A jewel is something precious, often knowledge extracted at great risk or personal treasures (qualities or abilities) you will uncover. In a dream, jewelry may be anything of great value to you. Alternatively, jewelry in dreams may symbolize greed, and wearing jewelry may suggest a craving for attention. Specific gems have individual symbolism: *diamonds* often stand for perfection, immortality, and light; *emeralds* symbolize growth; *pearls* represent beauty that results from suffering; *rubies* symbolize passion—love, as well as blood and violence; *sapphires* represent heaven, truth, and spirituality.

Joke

A good joke often makes fun of real life or puts something in a different and humorous light. Perhaps you need to re-examine a serious issue or laugh more and not take life so seriously.

Journey

A journey symbolizes discovery and change—growing and moving forward in life. It refers to ambition and aspiration—pursuing a goal, venturing on a quest (*see also* **Hero/Heroine**, **Knight**). Where are you going on your journey and what do you hope to accomplish? The journey is also related to **Flying**, **Running**, and **Swimming**.

Judge/Jury (*See also* **Trial**.)

Judges are authority figures who settle disputes, interpret laws, and impose sentences. What is the issue the jury faces in your dream? Perhaps conflict in a relationship has you seeking resolution. You may need help sorting through your options as you make a big decision. Or your conscience may be bothering you. This dream may also deal with justice. Do you feel you've been wronged?

Juggling

Do you have too many things going on in your life? Are you

trying to keep too many balls in the air? You may need to examine your priorities (decide what is important to you) and rearrange them to keep your life in balance. On the other hand, indecision may be making you keep your plans or options "up in the air."

Juice

Juice is the essence of its source. It relates to joy, energy, vitality, and health. But if you are "juicing" something, you may be draining it and sapping its strength.

Jungle (*See also* **Forest**.)

This dream may point to obstacles you face on the way to your goals. Do you have to whack through the foliage to clear a path? It may represent the harshness and confusion of a new and unfamiliar life situation: "It's a jungle out there." Might it be that unknown, even frightening, instinctual drives and feelings reside in that jungle?

K

Kettle

The kettle is where cooking culminates; all the preparation winds up there. A kettle may be where your energy transforms into something new, so it may represent creativity or the growth and development of your unique personality. At the same time, it may signal brewing trouble, as in a witch's cauldron or a "fine kettle of fish."

Key (*See also* **Lock**.)

What does the key open? It may be the solution to a problem or the crux of an issue. If you have a task to perform, the key may be the means to carrying it out. You may need to unlock hidden areas in your life to release your full potential. The key may be an opportunity; open the door and see what's on the other side. But the key may be cautioning you to do a better job keeping confidences; have you been blabbing someone's secrets? To lock something up and throw away the key is to put something out of reach and out of mind for good.

King

In dreams, a king may be a father figure and may reflect your feelings toward your dad. Dream kings also symbolize self-control, extreme awareness, and the rules that govern society. Do you follow the rules or do you tend to make up your own? Kings also represent achievement, victory, importance, and power. It may be that you feel like the "king (or **Queen**) of the castle."

Kiss

A kiss symbolizes close contact with another person, possibly even romance. Whom are you kissing? Does he or she represent someone else or some part of your self? A kiss has the power to break a spell and restore enchanted things and people to their proper shapes. Have you been bewitched? Other possible associations are respect, friendship, forgiveness, and betrayal.

Kitchen (See also **Cooking**.)

In practical terms, the kitchen is the "stomach" of the house where you eat; a kitchen in a dream may suggest that you examine the type and amount of food you consume. Are you eating healthfully? Does your diet give you the needed energy?

As a symbol, the kitchen is a place where creativity enables the preparation of delicious food and where the family gathers to share and enjoy it. In a dream, this may relate to the quality of family interaction, creative expression, or spiritual or emotional sustenance.

Kitten

See **Cat**.

Knife (See also **Sword**.)

A knife is an easily hidden weapon; the holder of a knife wields power. It can be used for both aggression and defense. A knife is a tool that can cut to the heart of an issue or cut away or clean out what is old or unneeded. To "stab someone in the back" is to betray him or her.

Knight (See also **Hero**/**Heroine**, **Journey**.)

Is your dream figure a "knight in shining armor" come to rescue you? Or is he on a quest—seeking adventure or treasure, or proving his (physical or spiritual) strength? As a symbol, the knight embodies superior physical and moral qualities. Are you striving for these yourself? It may require rigorous training, but it's worth it. A knight is shielded by armor; it can protect or it can hide him.

Knot (See also **Entanglement**.)

Knots represent complicated problems or relationships. If you are "tied up in knots," you may be anxious or unable to move. Find the center (the source of the trouble): you can untie the knot and break free. Knots are union, stability, and commitment; getting married is sometimes said to be "tying the knot." Remember, knots can also be cut through.

Kiss

L

Laboratory

If you have a science test coming up, then look no further for the dream's meaning. It may represent experimenting with new ideas and ways of seeing and dealing with life. What is the atmosphere in the lab? Is it cold and sterile or filled with volatile explosives? Or is it light, spacious, and well-equipped, conducive to free-ranging investigation? This may indicate how you approach your emotions.

Labyrinth

If you are lost in a labyrinth, you may be looking for a way out—to escape your worries. The key in this dream is to find the center (*see also* **Knot**); it holds the insight you need. The labyrinth is a symbol for the journey through the perils of life toward understanding and acceptance. A big part of life is simply trying to find direction.

Ladder

A ladder may symbolize ambition, "climbing to the top." It may be encouragement to reach higher for your goals. The ladder links the unconscious and the conscious. Are you climbing up or down?

Lamb

Lambs are associated with vulnerability, meekness, and gentleness. They may represent pure thought or a beginning. But the lamb also symbolizes sacrifice. Is something good being sacrificed—and for what reason?

Lamp (*See also* **Light**.)

A lamp provides light to conquer darkness: it brings problems to light and enables a better look at things; it gives reassurance, hope, and inspiration; it shows the way. The lamp represents intelligence, wisdom, and illumination of the mind and spirit.

Laughter

The free flow of events and associations in dreams can be very silly, even downright hilarious. Funny dreams may break an ongoing bad mood or help you cope during a difficult time. Enjoy the laughter and remember not to take life too seriously. Even dreams express the essential wisdom that humor helps; laughter *is* the best medicine. Dreams in which people are laughing at you may reflect feelings of embarrassment or inferiority.

Laundry

Laundry dreams may concern external appearances. Does something in your life need washing so you can look presentable? Perhaps there's something about which you need to "come clean" or you need to "clean up your act." "Airing dirty laundry" means exposing unflattering secrets.

Lead

As a base metal, lead may be the first or lowest stage in the transformation to something higher. It is a symbol of stubbornness, ignorance, and clumsiness. Have you been feeling dull or heavy? Maybe something is weighing on you. Lead is also poisonous. Are you in a harmful friendship or situation?

Leaf

A leaf is happiness; it signals growth and change. A tree with many leaves represents community or family. A green leaf connotes energy and willingness to achieve. A falling leaf indicates lack of direction or connection. Autumn leaves symbolize the end of a project or phase of life.

Lecture

If you are lecturing, you may want to make yourself understood, to get your point across. If you are being lectured to, it may be your conscience sending you a message. Are you ignoring people's warnings? Perhaps it is time to listen.

Leg

Legs provide the means to move, symbolizing motion, speed, energy, and victory. In dreams, the symbol can relate to progress along life's road. Do you feel confident to move forward on your own and take responsibility for yourself, to "stand on your own two feet"? Strong legs provide grounding, balance, and a good foundation. The condition of the legs may indicate your feelings about your ability to get where you want to go.

Lemon/Lemonade

Lemon, sour—the association is automatic. Has a friendship or situation in your life gone bad? This dream may suggest worthlessness, as in a car that is a "lemon." On the other hand, it may be encouragement to make opportunities ("lemonade") from those situations that at first seem harsh or irritating. Could you harbor some healthy, justified anger or resentment?

Lemonade is a natural progression from lemon. Your life may seem full of problems, but this

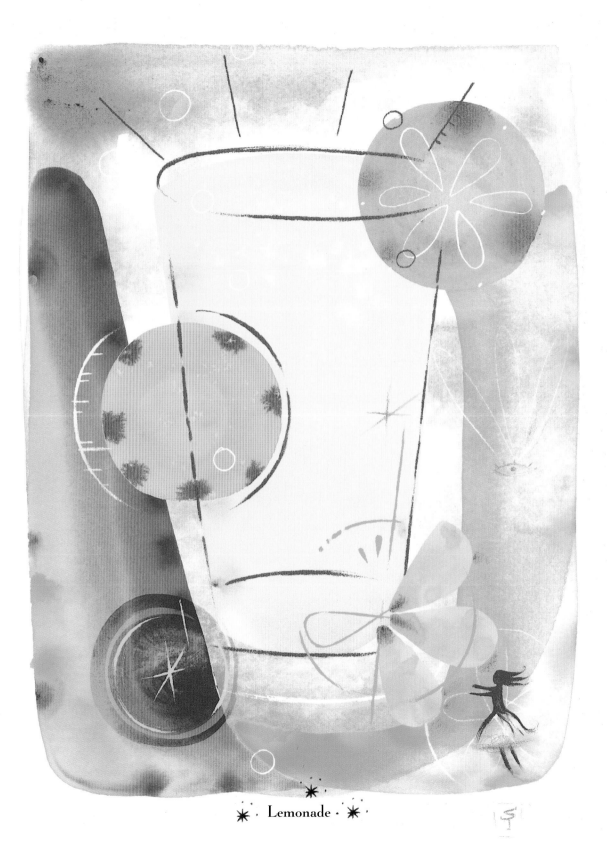

✳ · Lemonade · ✳

dream may help you figure out how to handle them. Make the best of whatever life hands you.

Letter

Who sent it and what the letter says may be keys to interpreting this dream. A letter represents connection with people; you may need to work on communicating with others. Are you withdrawn? Is your unconscious sending you a message? Pay attention.

Library

The library in your dream may be a source of accumulated wisdom, experience, and knowledge. You may have untapped intellectual resources. Or the dream may relate to an upcoming **Exam**.

Lie

See **Lying**.

Light

Light is purity, morality, optimism, belief, hope, and joy. It also represents the intellect, knowledge, and wisdom (things that lead you to "enlightenment"). The dream may be shedding light on a problem or question or providing you with the wisdom to solve it. It may be illuminating your creativity. Light is the opposite of depression, doubt, and illness. Perhaps this dream offers guidance out of a dark and troubled place. Are you being "blinded by the light"?

Lightning

A flash of lightning may signify a brilliant insight or inspiration, or sudden awareness. In mythology, lightning was seen as a message from the gods and being struck by lightning was considered an honor. Lightning can also symbolize power or wrath, in both nature and humans. Perhaps you harbor anger that you want to express in fierce aggression or a blinding burst of energy. A lightning bolt may signify an emotional shock.

Lion

As king of the jungle, the lion is nobility, strength, vigilance, fierceness, and pride. A lion may represent a father or authority figure or issues of power and domination. In many ancient cultures, the lion was symbolic of the **Sun**. A lion chasing you (*see also* **Chase**) may symbolize a thing that threatens you. What in your life reminds you of a lion? "Surviving the lion's den" means facing and overcoming danger.

Lock (*See also* **Key**.)

Are you locked out or in? Is something shut away that needs to be released? It may be feelings or parts of your self that you have trouble accepting (that you keep "locked up"). A lock may reflect the tension between taking a risk and feeling secure.

Loneliness

Feeling lonely in a dream may reflect real feelings of isolation, abandonment, or rejection. Examine whether your friendships feel right and satisfying. If you feel lonely in a crowd, you may not truly know or like yourself.

Lost

Being lost: This may express your feeling lost in everyday life—be it at school or with friends, in a new life or family situation, or in a spiritual sense. Ask yourself if anything in your waking life causes these same feelings of being lost. Pay attention to this dream; it may offer a clue to "finding yourself."

Losing something valuable: A valuable object often represents a person or identity, a thought or feeling, a dream or talent. Has anything in your life gone missing? You may be unclear about your place or importance in life.

Lottery

The lottery is a game of chance; playing it may symbolize taking a risk or avoiding responsibility. If you are hesitant to act, the dream may be encouraging you to take a chance. Or it may be cautioning you to give extra thought to your actions or decisions, to get more information. Don't trust in fate. Perhaps you have big dreams but don't know how to realize them.

Louse/Lice

Has a pest or parasite invaded your life? Do you know someone who's a louse? This dream may indicate feelings of disgust that you cannot easily escape. Do you harbor guilt or feel unclean in some way? Consider how you feel about your hair. Are you feeling lousy?

Luggage

Luggage holds your "stuff." In a dream, this may be emotional burdens, attitudes, or responsibilities, or simply your clothes and makeup. Do you carry emotional baggage? What have you packed and why? If you are in an unhappy situation, is it time to pack your bags and go? Luggage also represents travel. Are you taking a trip? It may be time for an adventure.

Lying

Your conscience may be troubling you. You may be living in falsehood or leading a double life. It may be time to 'fess up and tell the truth. This dream may be offering you the opportunity to be honest with yourself and others. Perhaps someone else is lying to you.

M

Machine/Machinery

You may feel like a machine, doing the same boring tasks over and over; your behaviors or attitudes may have become automatic, without thought or spontaneity. Has your life become routine and monotonous? The dream may point to work being done by your subconscious, your intellect, or your body; it may refer to a habit. A breakdown in the machinery may symbolize an obstacle in completing your work or a problem in your life.

Magician

A magician mediates between two opposing perceptions (reality and illusion, conscious and unconscious). Are you fooling yourself about something or suddenly seeing it as it really is? Has someone pulled a "disappearing act"? A dream magician may represent supernatural powers that can "fix" things or make dreams come true. You may have newly emerging talents or qualities awaiting recognition. Your own uniqueness contributes to your magic.

Mall (*See also* **Shopping**.)

The mall is a symbol of your social life—a place where you hang out with friends and check out what's happening. This dream may show your feelings about your social life and how dependent you are upon it. If the mall is filled with friends, you probably feel popular, lively, and fun. If the mall is deserted, you may be lonely.

It is also at the mall where shopping can satisfy a great many emotional needs. What are you buying? If you're on a shopping rampage, you may be trying hard to impress other people.

Man (*See also* **Stranger**.)

This dream may refer to a **Father** figure or one of authority or guidance. If a stranger, the man may be an aspect of your personality that isn't well known. If you know the man, he more than likely represents an issue or feeling about the

Mall

actual individual. What is he doing? Is there anyone in your life or any part of yourself that is like him?

Map

Just as in life, a dream map can show where you are going; it offers you direction and a clear path to follow. Are you facing a big decision? The map may provide help in choosing which way to go.

Marriage (See also Engagement, Wedding.)

Did you get engaged or married in your dream? This may suggest romance or signal your maturing as the parts of your personality come together. You may want the person you are marrying (your "other half") to fulfill your desires and meet your needs instead of doing the work yourself.

Mask (See also Disguise.)

The mask may be an image you present to others; why are you wearing it? Is it effective? You may be hiding who you really are, maybe because you don't really like yourself. If someone else is wearing a mask, perhaps you are being deceived. A mask can also symbolize impersonation and transformation. If you're disguised as someone whose qualities you

admire, you may hope to develop those qualities yourself.

Maze

See Labyrinth.

Meat

Do you eat meat? This dream may suggest that you are hungry or that your body is lacking some important nutrients. Meat symbolizes physical and creative power and raw, untamed emotion.

Medal

If you are in a competition, this dream may be unconscious preparation for it. The dream may deal with being praised and rewarded by others and may express a desire to win. Let your dream be encouragement to go for it.

Medication

This dream may point to emotional or physical need. The medication in the dream may suggest that you can "heal" from whatever is bothering you if you "take your medicine" and do what you need to do. It may concern retaliation, getting a "taste of your own medicine."

Messenger

Are you receiving a message? Pay attention, it may be important. If you are the messenger, you may have something important to communicate. If you are carrying messages between people, you may be stuck in the middle of a fight.

Milk

Milk is the basic, elemental food; it is equally symbolic of mother-love and nurturing. Does something in your life need nourishment? Milk also represents knowledge, insight, and human kindness. A land flowing with milk and honey is a symbol of paradise.

Mirror

The mirror is an important dream symbol; it shows what can't normally be seen. It may represent a deeper awareness of your inner self or your soul. Pay attention to the reflected image; it may help establish your identity and your importance as an individual. On a more superficial level, the reflection may show how you see yourself or how you want others to see you. If you see someone else's reflection in the mirror, perhaps you are trying to be someone you aren't. The mirror may symbolize transformation, change, vanity, or pride.

Model

A person: The appearance of a fashion model in your dream may deal with feelings—often insecurities—about your body or your beauty, or a preoccupation with your appearance, your clothes, or your social status. It may suggest pleasure in being the focus of flattering attention.

An object: As a scaled-down (smaller) version of a thing, it may reduce a situation, problem, or issue to a size you can handle. If you build scale models, the dream may just refer to your hobby.

Mole

The animal: Something deep inside you may be urging you to examine your unconscious drives and beliefs. Are you snooping around in other people's business? Are you keeping secrets of your own? It may be time to shed some light on them.

A beauty mark: Such a mark can be very distinctive; it's practically a trademark for Marilyn Monroe. For this reason, it is often a symbol of recognition. At the same time, it's often a feature on the face of a witch in fairy tales. Who bears the mark in your dream and what feelings does it arouse?

Money

Money in dreams generally relates to internal resources such as self-esteem, intelligence, emotional strength, and creative energy—your rich uniqueness. A dream of losing money may follow the death or departure of someone important to you, reflecting not only the loss of the loved one but of the qualities you value in that person. Here, the dream is helping you grieve; it is part of the healing process, however unwelcome it may seem. Other loss dreams—of a purse or backpack—may reflect concerns about your purpose or identity, especially if a dream or goal has recently been thwarted.

Monkey

See **Ape**.

Monster

A monster in a dream may symbolize an individual in your life or some energy, emotion, or quality in you that seems to threaten or overpower you. It may be strong feelings that are becoming more than you can handle or some quality or tendency in yourself (or someone else) that you find ugly or frightening. The monster may represent a moral or emotional conflict with which you are struggling. Keep in mind that this pent-up energy also has enormous creative possibility.

Moon

The ocean's tides are affected by the moon's cycles. The cycle starts with the new moon, relating to potential, and ends with the full moon, symbolizing completion. Shifting or extreme emotions and irrational impulses are sometimes attributed to these cycles; the word "lunatic" derives from the Latin word for moon. The moon signals nighttime and rest. Moonlight is associated with romance; vintage love songs include such lyrics as "the magic of moonlight" and "by the light of the silvery moon."

Mother

Generally, dream mothers symbolize nurturing, protection, love, support, or self-discipline. As a young woman, it may also refer to your own basic feminine nature or qualities. If your actual mother shows up in your dream, it may reflect issues or interaction with her. The action and overall feeling in the dream may be keys to its deeper message.

Mountain

By dint of its height and what can be seen from its top, a mountain may symbolize a higher view or awareness, a towering achievement (or the aspiration to it), or divine wisdom or spiritual understanding. At the same time, a mountain may represent an imposing obstacle. Climbing a mountain suggests facing problems and overcoming hardship.

Mouse

Cartoons abound with mice, and not just Mickey, Minnie, and Mighty. They are often clever; though small and seemingly insignificant, they manage to outwit far larger and more powerful opponents. They symbolize the weak overcoming the strong. Mice may also be humble, quiet, poor, and timid. A dream featuring a plague of mice may hint at numerous small but annoying problems.

Mouth

The mouth is an instrument of speech and self-expression; it signifies the power of the spoken word. It is a means of connecting and communicating with others. But if you have a "big mouth," you may be talking too much or blurting things you shouldn't. Your words may be hurting others. It's also closely connected with eating and taking things into the body. Do you hunger for something? Do you feel obliged to "swallow" something unwholesome or disagreeable?

Mud

Mud is dirty, slippery, and yucky. It may symbolize anything with similar qualities, including feelings or situations. In a dream, being stuck in mud may symbolize being mired in problems. "Mudslinging" means damaging a reputation. Someone who is conservative or old-fashioned is a "stick-in-the-mud."

Mummy

The dream mummy may represent an attitude or behavior that is no longer appropriate, or an idea or obligation that "died" a long time ago but continues to have a hold on you. It may deal with feeling immobilized or unable to act effectively in some real-life situation.

Music

Music is associated with inner peace, balance, and harmony. It represents self-expression and the free flow of emotions. What is the music in your dream? Music can dispel sadness; perhaps your dream is helping lighten your spirit. Or it may suggest anxiety about suffering a consequence (as in "facing the music").

♑

Nakedness

Ever dream about going outside in the buff or of having your clothes fall off in the middle of school? The people in your dream may respond by laughing hysterically or by being oddly indifferent. Either way, it's uncomfortable and acutely embarrassing. In a dream, appearing naked in public may reflect anxiety about being exposed or criticized ("found out"). You may feel unprepared for something or afraid to reveal your feelings. If, on the other hand, you are not embarrassed, it may be that you are at ease with yourself, that you are open and honest.

Does the setting in your dream correspond to anything in your life? Do others care that you are naked? If not, perhaps you don't really have anything to be embarrassed about. Dreams of public nudity may reflect new roles and evolving identity as you mature.

Names

"What's in a name?" A great deal. Names are symbols. Names define and categorize, they give identity. A name is the essence of a thing or person. What is the name in the dream and what does it mean to you? Names can reveal how we really feel about ourselves and others. Puns in the name may be messages from your unconscious.

Neck

The neck is a symbol of strength, stubbornness, will power, and self-restraint. It symbolizes the mind-body connection. The neck allows or prohibits expression of intellect and feelings. Do you choke back your feelings? Do you speak them too strongly? Perhaps you are "sticking your neck out."

Pain in the neck or throat may signal a real-life sore throat. It may be someone who is bothering you, being a "pain in the neck." Having something stuck in your throat means having difficulty finding the words you need to say.

Needle

If you dream of needles you may be anxious about something ("on pins and needles"), annoyed by minor irritations that "needle" you, or feeling either emotional or physical pain. As a tool in sewing, a needle can create, decorate, and repair items made of fabric. You may be putting something together creatively.

Neighbor

Does the dream neighbor suggest personal traits of a real neighbor or of similar (or desired) qualities within you? It may also refer to compassion or helpfulness.

Net (*See also* **Entanglement**.)

Nets gather, hold, and confine things. Dreaming of one may point to feeling somehow trapped. Is there something you are trying to escape? The net may also represent entangled ideas or instincts. Do your thoughts or feelings control you, or do you hold them back?

You may also be trying to understand an issue. Remember, a safety net is a net, too—and a good thing to have around in case you fall.

New Room

See **Room**.

Newspaper

Do you need to pay more attention to what's going on in the world? The message here may be that you should focus more on the world outside—or inside, at important emotional developments. It may be pushing you to express yourself more openly, to put yourself out there. Look for puns in the headlines or section titles of the paper.

Night

Night may represent sleep, darkness, or the unconscious or hidden parts of your self. If you can find your way around at night or see in the dark, you may be mastering your feelings, learning effectively to deal with issues coming from the unconscious. If you are stumbling around, you may be resisting parts of your self that are working to emerge.

Nightmare

Nightmares always concern something fearful or disturbing. It may be conflict, stress, or discomfort in any part of your life: past or present, real or imagined, home or school, family or society in general, world events or those at home. The way you feel about issues or events in any of these areas and the way you handle them (or choose not to) may come through in your dreams.

Because nightmares provoke strong emotional reactions, they are generally better remembered than ordinary dreams. Nightmares get your attention, and for good reason: they are telling you what's really on your mind. Don't let them scare you. Examining and understanding your nightmares will give you insight into areas you may have been avoiding; you can begin to identify those issues and perhaps even find ways to deal with them. Try to be objective; you have the intellectual power to pick apart the dream even if it feels scary. If it becomes too uncomfortable, stop. You can always come back to it later. Analyze the different symbols as you would those in any other dream. What you discover may be priceless.

Noise

It may be that you are incorporating real noise into your dream, such as the sound of your alarm clock. Or your life may feel busy, cluttered, or overwhelming.

Nose

Have you been meddling in other people's business? Perhaps you're being nosy. Looking down your nose means acting like a snob. A good nose denotes good instincts; you may want to follow it.

Nudity

See **Nakedness**.

Number (*See also* **Four**.)

Does the number in your dream correspond to a significant year, date, or time of day; number of people; or address? Perhaps it indicates your age when something important happened to you. Individual numbers have their own meanings.

Zero may suggest nothingness or meaninglessness.

One is unity or a starting point, an "on your mark" signal.

Two represents symmetry or the union of opposites (heaven and earth, man and woman).

Three represents a triangle or trio and the elements of mind, body, spirit.

Four signifies four corners and so represents stability, the earth, and the seasons.

Five stands for health, the body, and the hand.

Six is the symbol for the soul.

Seven is the number of completeness and perfect order.

Eight represents infinity, wholeness, grounding. It is also an octave in music.

Nine symbolizes new or renewal and eternity.

Nurse (*See also* **Doctor**, **Hospital**.)

A nurse gives nurturing and comfort, somewhat like a mother. A dream nurse may offer warmth and healing attention. Allow her to help. If, on the other hand, you are the nurse, you may be perfectly able to take care of yourself.

O

Oasis

An oasis is a lush, restful garden that interrupts the arid desert. It is fed by water from deep underground. Water being symbolic of the unconscious, an oasis may suggest emerging thoughts and feelings. An oasis may offer a pause or break from the usual labor or routine.

Oath

An oath is a solemn promise made before witnesses. Before testifying in court, witnesses take an oath to tell the truth. In a dream, it may suggest a commitment. Oaths remain dependable when a lot of other things in life may feel unstable or insecure.

Obstacle

Obstacles in dreams often mirror obstacles in life, whether real or imagined, conscious or unconscious. It may be a barrier that is internal and self-imposed, such as inhibitions and attitudes, or external, such as class requirements. What kind of obstacle is it? A person, a natural feature (a tree or boulder), or something man made (an age limit)? Examining this is the key to understanding and overcoming whatever has been keeping you from making progress.

Ocean

All life derives from the ocean, which is thus a symbol of the unconscious and all that originates there: emotions, intuition, potential—the whole of everyone's inner truth. A stormy sea suggests the upheaval caused by buried thoughts or feelings rising toward the surface (into awareness). A calm sea implies serenity and peace. Traveling across the ocean represents a **Journey** or growth.

Octopus

Do you need more arms to get everything done? Are you reaching out and grabbing to get more "stuff"? Perhaps you feel caught up in or entangled by someone or something. The octopus is related to the **Spider Web**.

Odor (*See also* **Perfume**.)

What is that smell? Is it something pleasing and delicious or is it rank and disgusting? A bad smell may signal that something is rotten.

Officer

See **Police Officer**.

Oil

Oil is wealth taken from the earth. It symbolizes energy, as it was once burned to provide light and is the basis for gasoline and fuel. It lubricates metals and machines. Some oils are healing balms that restore smoothness to the skin and anoint. At the same time, oil can be destructive; a spill that threatens wildlife is shameful environmental pollution. "Oily" also describes untrustworthy people.

Operation (*See also* **Doctor**, **Hospital**, **Nurse**.)

A surgical operation removes, repairs, replaces, or implants something in the body. Does this apply to any part of you, emotional or physical? The procedure may be painful, but in the end it will bring healing and relief.

Orchestra (*See also* **Band**.)

An orchestra comprises people working to create harmony, to make "beautiful music together." Perhaps this is your hope for relationships with friends and family. It may apply as well to the different facets of your personality. If there is discord, then someone (or something within you) may be out of tune or rhythm. Of course, this dream may also represent rehearsal for an upcoming concert.

Ostrich

An ostrich is (falsely) said to bury its head in the sand when it senses threat or danger, so it has become a symbol for denial. It likewise symbolizes forgetfulness and willful lack of understanding. The ostrich is one of those birds that cannot fly; perhaps you have been preparing for something but aren't yet ready.

Oven

The oven is a symbol of transformation (growth or change). What do you have "cooking"? Conversely, you may be under pressure or feeling the heat. Be assured that something healthy and fulfilling will soon emerge.

Owl

The owl symbolizes wisdom. And because an owl can see in the dark, it may bring insight into a problem or hints on how to deal with it.

P

Package (*See also* **Gift**.)

What is in the package? It may be anything from intellectual or emotional gifts (skills, resources, talents) to emotional burdens (fears or anxieties) that are hidden away or under wraps. Open it up and see what's inside: it may lead to greater understanding of yourself. If the package is a gift, think about who gave it to you. Is it something you are giving to someone else?

Palace

A palace symbolizes the comfort, security, and wealth of royalty; in earlier times, those occupants in the dungeon may have suffered isolation and imprisonment. Do you have the run of the palace or are you being held in the dungeon or some high turret? You may want to be treated like a princess, to feel recognized and appreciated. The secret chambers in the palace may be the unconscious; treasure hidden there symbolizes internal riches or spiritual truth. Fairy tale palaces may represent escape into imagination, into a story that has a happy ending.

Pants (*See also* **Clothes**, **Nakedness**.)

Pants may symbolize self-determination and authority, as in the expression to "wear the pants in the family." Being without pants exposes you and makes you vulnerable. If you get caught "with your pants down," you may feel unprepared, embarrassed, or ashamed.

Paper

Paper with writing on it may be a message, much like a **Book**. Blank paper may signify emotions not yet expressed (a story yet unwritten), a lack of awareness of them, or a lack of desire to express them. Blank pages offer a fresh start on a creative project. Paper may reflect thoughts about an upcoming test or report.

Parachute (*See also* **Falling**, **Flying**.)

A dream parachute may be offering help and protection—a soft landing—in some risky endeavor. Falling gently through the air suggests feelings of playfulness or inhibition that may lead to creativity. A parachute that doesn't open may hint at fear that those you rely on for help and support are going to let you down.

Parade

Parades offer a good time for everyone involved, participant and spectator alike. They are occasions on which to lose inhibitions, show off a little, and attract admiring attention. A parade may represent a special time, achievement, or recognition in your life. If you "rain on" someone else's parade, you may be jealous of their success.

Paradise

Paradise is a symbol of pristine happiness, a state in which your every need is satisfied. A dream of paradise may allude to running away from real-life burdens or responsibilities, escaping to a time or place more comfortable and carefree. Paradise is that elusive state of being—representing inner peace and self-acceptance—in which you have achieved all your goals and desires. Conversely, a paradise dream may simply be a momentary stay, a time-out from your ordinary existence.

Paralysis (*See also* **Help, inability to call for**, **Running**.)

Paralysis is the inability to move, symbolizing helplessness or a failure or reluctance to act or decide or to function effectively. The cause may be fear of the consequences, conflict, or guilt. You may feel inadequate or anxious about an upcoming test.

Are you feeling mentally or emotionally frozen? Are you holding something back?

Parent (*See also* **Father**, **Mother**, **Family**.)

Parents in a dream may represent actual parents (or other parental figures) or aspects (characteristics) of your parents or issues you have with them. Parents in dreams may symbolize people you trust, from whom you seek or accept help or advice. If you are having conflict with your parents, this dream may be offering help to resolve it. A dream parent may signify love, nurturing, discipline, or authority.

Park (*See also* **Garden**.)

The park is a symbol of nature tamed, wildness controlled, yet retaining the restful beauty of the natural environment. A park in your dream offers a place to get away, to relax, play, and have fun.

Parrot

The parrot may be a symbol of mindless chatter. Have you been gossiping? Could others be telling secrets or talking behind your back? Perhaps you have been repeating what others say without giving it real thought.

Party

Are you enjoying the party in the dream? Are you surrounded by friends and laughter—or is the party quiet and dull? The party atmosphere may represent how you feel about your social life and about your own happiness and well-being. The dream may be telling you that you need to lighten up and take life less seriously—or that you are too much the party animal; perhaps you need to buckle down and get serious about things.

Peacock

A strutting peacock fanning out its extravagant tail feathers may symbolize arrogance or vanity; a contrary interpretation may be undue modesty or reserve. Are you showing off or overly concerned about how others see you? Perhaps you are a shining star disguised as a wallflower.

Pearl (See also **Jewelry**.)

Created in the ocean depths, pearls represent gifts from the unconscious, often those of female insight and intuition (as in "pearls of wisdom"). The pearl symbolizes making a problem into a thing of beauty and value, as an oyster does the irritant that causes it to form a pearl. The pearl also symbolizes purity and wealth. If the pearls are broken, you may not trust your instincts.

Pen/Pencil

Writing instruments are symbols of self-expression, used to create and communicate. Pens preserve ideas and events and also relate to power ("the pen is mightier than the sword"). It may be that this dream is suggesting you write something down; it may reflect thoughts about a paper or an upcoming test.

Performance (See also **Actor**, **Audience**.)

When you perform in public, people's attention centers on you, whether critical or kind. Are you afraid of criticism or seeking praise? Be careful not to get too focused on yourself. Are you rehearsing for a performance in real life?

Perfume (See also **Odor**.)

One use for perfume is to mask the smell of something unpleasant. Could you be trying to "throw someone off the scent"? Of course, it's also used to attract flattering attention. In any case, the dream deals with sensory stimulation.

Pearl

Person/People (*See also* **Family**, **Famous People**, **Friend**, **Stranger**.)

Multitudes of people can appear in dreams—some you know and some are complete strangers. In dreams, people you know represent aspects of your relationship with them or certain qualities you admire in them. Strangers may symbolize aspects of your self— your attitudes or the way you see yourself, or your emotional state. What does the person mean to you? Does the number of people have any special meaning?

Photograph/Photography (*See also* **Camera**.)

A photograph preserves an image; it may be an attempt to keep something from the past unchanged. If the photo is of yourself, perhaps you need to see yourself in a different light or become more aware of who you are. Pictures of your family or others in your life may suggest you look more closely at them. If you are taking pictures, you may need a more objective view of something; the dream may be a call to focus your attention and see things clearly.

Physician
See **Doctor**.

Piano

Playing the piano creates melody and harmony; it's a cultural expression that enlivens any gathering. Piano music may represent emotions that are coming to the surface. Disharmony (discord) or a piano out of tune may point to some area in your life that needs adjustment (or "tuning"). The dream may refer to an upcoming recital or competition. Use the dream to practice handling your nerves.

Pig

The pig is often seen as rude, sloppy, greedy, and lazy, any of which qualities this dream may suggest. Do any of these uncivilized behaviors pertain to you? "Pig-headed" is another word for stubborn. "Acting like a pig" hints at impolite behavior.

Pill
See **Medicine**.

Pirate

Pirates attack and plunder; they symbolize adventure and defiance of authority. But those they attack may suffer loss and emotional injury; they can be thrown off course and into danger. Have you lost something of value?

Poet

The classic image of the poet is romantic and idealistic, but also creative and inspired. How do you feel about these qualities? Do you have to write a poem for school? Your brain may be working on it.

Police Officer

Police deal with enforcement of laws, maintenance of order and control, public safety and protection, and issues of guilt, and so do dreams about them. Dream police may represent parental or authority figures or issues concerning respect. They may suggest a conflict with ordinary rules. Are you having trouble at school? This dream may also represent your conscience. Are you feeling guilt? This dream may also show a desire for more limits, order, authority, or protection in your life, whether self-imposed or set by parents or other adults.

Pond

See **Ocean**.

Porcupine

The porcupine protects and defends himself by straightening his quills so they point outward. Have you been feeling prickly because of some annoyance or intrusion? Perhaps you are trying to protect or isolate yourself. What is it that's bothering you?

Prince/Princess

Royalty are generally important people treated with respect and honor. In a dream, they represent the dreamer and may hint at issues surrounding stature or place in society. This dream may signal your growing command of yourself as you move toward independence and maturity. But if you are bossy or demanding in the dream, you may be acting like a "spoiled princess." Are you a fairy tale princess in need of a rescue?

Prison/Prisoner

Many situations can feel like being in prison: strict limitations on time or activity set by parents or teachers; intense relationships that stifle personal growth or expression; failure to act caused by your own fears or inhibitions; guilt that hangs you up, whether justified or not. Some of these are prisons of your own making and others are forced upon you. If you prevent yourself from taking risks or trying new things, it may be time to break out. If the "prison" is imposed, examine why and whether it may be a good thing.

Privacy (*See also* **Bathroom**.)

There are some things you must simply do in private. If you dream of having difficulty finding a place to take a shower, change clothes, or go to the bathroom away from others, you may be suffering a lack of privacy. You may need to find some space or time to call your own, without interruption or intrusion. You may be shy or anxious about opening up to others. Are you preparing to talk to a group?

Puppet

A puppet is controlled by strings or by a hidden hand. Do you have a relationship like this? Are you the puppet or the puppeteer? Perhaps you are in a situation with strings attached, where your power is limited. You may feel somehow dependent.

Puzzle

A dream puzzle may represent a mental challenge, a problem you need to solve. Putting the right pieces together may resolve a complicated situation. If clues or pieces are missing, you may not have all the information you need.

Q

Quarantine

Quarantine is a precaution to stop the spread of contagious disease by keeping sick people away from others. This dream may represent feelings of illness or isolation, of having limited access to people or information. You may feel alone or separated from friends or family or shut out by someone in your life. Or are you banishing some part of your self? Perhaps you have a secret you fear may infect others.

Quarrel (*See also* **Fight**.)

This dream may represent a conflict within your self or with others, or hidden anger or resentment toward yourself or someone close to you. Are you in an argument? Does the dream offer any insight into resolving it?

Queen (*See also* **King**, **Mother**.)

Queens are women with power and authority, and they symbolize these things in a dream. These qualities reside in you, too; they are your nature, instincts, and intuition—the feminine forces in your personality. In a dream, a queen may also represent the idea of mother, or your actual mother.

Quicksand

Quicksand is deceptive; it has the appearance of ordinary sand, but can pull you in and trap you. In a dream, this may symbolize being tricked or wandering unknowingly into danger. You may feel stuck or overwhelmed, helpless or inadequate. What is it that holds you?

Quiet (*See also* **Noise**.)

Quiet characterizes peace and serenity, things that may help you to relax and think. You might enjoy having more of this quality in your life—or do you have too much? An eerie silence may come before a calamity, as in the "quiet before the storm." Are you anticipating something that makes you anxious? Perhaps you feel stifled by a warning to "keep quiet."

Quilt

A quilt is a blanket or coverlet made from separate small pieces of fabric lovingly stitched together in a carefully designed pattern. It may symbolize the transformation of the separate growing parts of your personality into a mature whole. It calls to mind the family culture and wisdom that, like a quilt, is passed down from one generation to the next. Of course, a quilt also suggests warmth, covering, and protection.

Quiz (*See also* **Exam**.)

If you dream of a "pop quiz," it may be that you anticipate a problem or test of some kind. You may feel unprepared for something you have to do or you may have a sense of inadequacy about something. If you dream that you do well on the quiz, you have the right attitude and expectation for success.

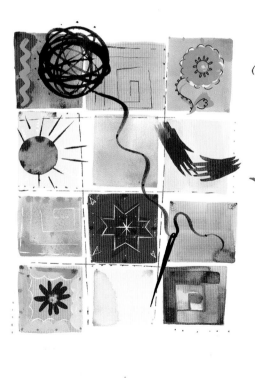

R

Rabbit

Rabbits are characterized as fast-multiplying animals, sometimes cartoonishly. They are timid and vulnerable, reliant on their watchfulness and speed to avoid danger. Rabbits are easily preyed upon and made victims, even as their soft fur and large ears give them charm and appeal. It may be these qualities that place them in your dream. Consider how you feel about your dream rabbit. Do you identify with it in any way? A rabbit's foot is a token of good luck.

Racing

Races measure many things, among them speed, skill, ambition, and competitiveness. A dream race deals with feelings about these things, as well as about winning and losing; it may relate to your levels of stress, energy, and self-esteem. Do you measure yourself against others? Are you racing against time? This dream may reflect feelings about your schoolwork, sports participation, or extracurricular activity. The dream may indicate your ambition as well as how you feel about competing and your ability to succeed.

Radio (*See also* **Music**, **Messenger**.)

If the radio is sending you a message, what is playing or who is speaking? What you hear on a dream radio is often your own thoughts and feelings, so pay attention to the announcements and song lyrics. Jamming to a radio may mean that you feel ready to cut loose and have fun.

Railroad (*See also* **Train**.)

Railroad dreams suggest a journey, possibly the journey through life. It may signify a crossroad, a chance to change your destination. Do you need to change trains and head in a different direction? Have you lost track of your goals or ambitions? Missing the train may symbolize losing out on an opportunity. The dream may also signify being on the right track, or getting off track.

Rain

With the rain comes a release of tension; whether a cleansing shower or a torrential downpour. Rain is a symbol of purification, inspiration, fertility, and renewal. It may represent mourning, introspection, or thwarted plans; did someone or something "rain on your parade"? Perhaps something in your life feels gray and stormy.

Rainbow

A rainbow is created when sun and rain come together; it is a symbol of harmony, peace, wholeness, blessing, and transition. It may signal that you have weathered the storm and your troubles are at an end. Folklore holds that there is gold at the end of the rainbow; you may feel rewarded for all your hard work.

Rat

Rats are aggressive, destructive pests that spread disease. They inhabit dark, dirty places and are considered filthy, sneaky, and untrustworthy. Are you having nagging thoughts or doubts? If you are beginning to have suspicions, you are "smelling a rat." A rat is a friend who treats you badly or abandons you in a crisis. An informer who spills your secrets is "ratting on you" or is "ratting you out."

Raven (See also **Bird**.)

Perhaps because of their characteristic black color, ravens may bring negative fantasies or thoughts or bad luck, as in Edgar Allan Poe's poem, "The Raven." In any case, they represent messengers, and sometimes, guardians.

Red

Red represents vitality, passion, and action, and feelings of anger, embarrassment, and vengeance. Red is the color of blood and fire and may warn of danger. What in your dream is colored red?

Referee

The referee symbolizes fairness, "following the rules" when dealing with the world and with your self. Think about how you play the game. If you've been taking cheap shots and causing fouls, the referee may be a symbol to clean up your act. If a friend has been treating you unfairly, it may be time to right those wrongs.

Refrigerator (See also , **Ice**.)

A refrigerator stores and chills **Food**. Are you in an emotional freeze or putting something "on ice" for the time being? Is there a situation in your life in which you need to "play it cool"? You may feel overheated by stress or anxiety. Try to slow down and "chill out."

Rejection (*See also* **Abandonment**.)

This dream may deal with feelings about being abandoned, left out, or not being good enough. It may tap into feelings of self-worth as they relate to approval or acceptance by friends or family (or yourself). This dream may be telling you not to worry—you are valuable just as you are. If it's you rejecting something or someone, it's important to identify what it is and why you are rejecting it; it may a bad habit that you legitimately need to break, but it may also be some essential part of your self.

Relatives

See **Family**.

Report Card

Yikes! How are your grades? Your dream may express anxiety about them, whether you have just received your report card or your grades are soon to be given. You may be evaluating your performance in school or in life overall. Good grades may confirm how well you feel you are doing; poor grades may represent criticism or disapproval.

Rescue

Dreaming of rescue is a way of coping with difficult situations or people in real life. If you are often the rescuer, you may be overly concerned with pleasing others or the one people always turn to for help. If you are being rescued, you may feel helpless or overwhelmed in some area of your life and wish that someone would offer you a hand. The person being rescued may be some part of yourself that you are coming to acknowledge or accept. Remember, both the rescuer and the rescued in your dream may represent aspects of your personality. You have it in you to save yourself.

Restaurant

This dream may symbolize social interaction, time spent with family or friends, intellectual stimulation, exchange of information, decision making, and obviously, eating. If the experience is positive, it suggests quality time with family and friends who help you feel nurtured and energized. But if the meal is unpleasant, you may feel uncomfortable or superficial. Watching others eat and having no food of your own may represent feelings of neglect or of being taken for granted.

Ribbon

Ribbons represent awards or achievements; first prize is often a blue ribbon. Ribbons decorate gifts, demonstrate support, and symbolize friendship ("the ties that bind") and girlish pleasures (ribbons and curls). Ceremonies inaugurating new projects or ships often feature a ribbon cutting.

Riddle (*See also* **Knot**, **Puzzle**.)

Riddles make you think; they puzzle you and help you find answers.

Rifle

See **Weapon**.

Ring

The circle of a ring symbolizes wholeness and eternity. Worn on your finger, this circle represents an unbreakable bond or commitment. Rings are also symbols of power and recognition.

Riot

Are you being foolhardy in following the crowd? This dream may be questioning whether you are thinking for yourself. Make sure you know what you believe and why. Don't just take someone else's word for it. The noise and chaos of a riot may suggest confusion or disorder you may feel in some area of your life.

River (*See also* **Water**.)

As a ceaseless flow of water, a river may symbolize hope, fertility, energy, renewal, emotions, and life's **Journey**. A river is a barrier to the other side; cross it and you may change your life. Are you "going with the flow" or "swimming upstream?" A river also suggests cleansing.

Road

Like **River**, a road may represent life's **Journey**. It symbolizes your experience and the progress you are making. The road in your dream may tell something about your direction. Do you know where you are going? A fork in the road indicates a change or an upcoming decision.

Robber

See **Burglar**.

Robot

A robot is a machine that simulates a human being; however, it has the advantage of performing perfectly without thinking or feeling. Have you been functioning on automatic lately or been feeling dead inside? You may be depressed or, perhaps in some area of your life, you are not being real.

River/Road

Rock

Rocks symbolize stability, strength, and permanency. If someone in your dream is "solid as a rock," you can depend upon and trust that person. Rocks may also represent obstacles or difficulties to overcome. Perhaps you are being "hard-headed" and stubborn.

Roof

The roof is the top of the house and so may represent your head, your intelligence, or your thoughts. Perhaps you are seeking a new perspective. A roof provides shelter from rain and storms. In what condition is the roof? If it is sagging or full of holes, you may feel unprotected in some area.

Room

If in dreams you find new rooms in your house or school, you may be discovering new talents or areas of your life or personality to explore. This indicates growth and expansion; you may be developing into a more complex, more interesting person. What are the rooms? Do you enjoy being in them?

Rope

If the rope is tying someone up, it suggests being forced, bound, or somehow inhibited. Are you tied up or are you roping (controlling) someone else? Ropes are also used to help people to safety. In that case, they symbolize security and rescue. If you "know the ropes," you feel confident in a situation.

Rose

The rose is often considered the perfect flower or the queen of flowers. It symbolizes completion and perfection. It is also a symbol of the self and of wholeness (Jung). The rose is a flower of romance and love, inspiration, and wisdom.

Ruin

A ruin is something that has fallen into disrepair through disuse or neglect. Perhaps you have goals or dreams that you have abandoned. The ruins may also represent a neglected friendship.

Running (*See also* **Chase**, **Paralysis**.)

Being unable to run in a dream expresses frustration. Your legs may feel paralyzed; you may even come awake. This may reflect a situation in real life in which you feel somehow immobilized or helpless.

Running, tripping: We've all seen scary movies where the heroine is running frantically from danger when…*surprise*…she trips. These themes play out in dreams, too, and may be a variation on being unable to run. It may point to an obstacle or frustration in your life, something that holds you back. A lack of self-confidence? Your life may be too hurried or busy or you may not be taking the time to watch where you're going. You may run into physical or emotional hazards if you don't slow down and look out.

Running toward or away: Running toward or after something or someone may express ambition, confidence, a positive attitude, or initiative. Running away may be a means of fleeing danger, or it may reflect cowardice, guilt, or doubt about your ability to succeed. If you're "running around in circles," you're never going to get anywhere.

Running for exercise may mean you feel good about your life and the way it is going. You may be taking steps to improve your physical or emotional health. It may also be a mental rehearsal for an upcoming track event.

Rust

What is the object that is rusting? Something in your life may be deteriorating—a friendship you are neglecting or a personal quality or skill you are failing to use.

S

Sailboat

See **Boat**.

Sand

Countless grains of sand cover great expanses of beach and desert in ever-changing dunes and valleys. Sand may thus represent infinity (the number of grains), relaxing in the sun (the beach), or instability (the shifting dunes). Does something in your life have a shaky foundation? Do you need a vacation? Waves lapping at the sand may suggest the smoothing over of something rough. If a grain of sand symbolizes something in your dream, you may be placing too much importance on a small matter. Sand falling in an hourglass symbolizes the passing of time.

Savings (*See also* **Bank**.)

Dreams about savings may represent your inner reserves of strength, intelligence, talent, or potential. Your assets may be growing; in time, they will mature and you will be enriched. Alternatively, this dream may suggest anxiety about your emotional or financial security.

Saw

The saw may represent your ability to cut through obstacles and turn them into something useful. It is also a symbol of the industry, transformation, and willpower necessary to achieve success.

Scale

The scales of justice represent fairness, an element crucial in deciding such matters as guilt and punishment. Are you being treated unjustly in some way? Perhaps you aren't being fair to others. Is your conscience clear? The scale may indicate a matter of some importance, as in a "weighty issue"; it may also be a symbol of your personal power and influence. Is your life balanced and in order? As a symbol, a different take on the scale is its function to measure weight. Is this something that concerns you?

Scar

A scar remains after an **Injury** heals. Do you have an old wound from which you continue to suffer? It may be time for healing. Scars are also marks of identification.

School (*See also* **Exam**.)

A dream about school may simply reflect an experience you've had there, though it may be triggered by anxiety about something social, academic, or athletic. Dreams about school probably concern learning, making friends, and trying new things. What's important is what happens in the dream and your feelings about it.

Science (*See also* **Laboratory**.)

The science in your dream may represent a desire to experiment with solutions to a perplexing situation in your life. It may also be leading you to an important emotional or intellectual discovery. If you have an upcoming science test, the dream may be a way of processing your anxieties.

Scissors

As a cutting tool, a scissors may symbolize the loss of—or the need to cut away or separate from—a friendship or situation. Scissors cut and shape fabric in the process of making or altering clothing. Does something in your life call for change? Sarcasm or criticism can take the form of "cutting" remarks.

Scorpion

The most distinctive feature of the scorpion is its tail, equipped with a venomous sting that arches over its body, ever ready for attack or defense. As a symbol, the scorpion represents aggression, cynicism, pain and hurt, or negative thoughts. In a dream of a scorpion, you may be the scorpion itself or its victim. It may reflect a painful situation or the exchange of "stinging" remarks.

Scream
See **Help, inability to call for**.

Sculpture
If you regard the wood, clay, or stone as an obstacle, you may be overcoming it in the creative process of carving or molding. Perhaps you are shaping an original thought or cutting away the extraneous to reveal your essence. If the sculpture is of someone or something you recognize, take special note of the symbolism.

Sea
See **Ocean**.

Seed
First and foremost, a seed symbolizes fertility; from that idea flows potential, creativity, productivity, new insight, personal growth, and wisdom. Planting a seed may represent the unseen possibilities in a situation, person, or friendship. If the seed is nourished, it will grow.

Servant
A servant dream symbolizes a relationship in which the parties are not equal; one commands the other. The dream highlights one side or the other of this equation, serving another or being served; it may be arrogance—bossing others around—or humbleness—being "lorded over." Are you the servant or the master?

Sewing
This dream expresses creative energy; you are putting something together. It may be the parts of your self coming together into a mature personality. Your dream sewing may also be mending or transforming something.

Shark
The shark is a brutal and voracious predator, possibly symbolizing your own anger or hostility, or a person who is greedy, deceitful, or quick to strike.

Sheep
Sheep are rather docile creatures that follow along unthinkingly. Have you been conforming to a group, accepting their ideas or behavior without question? Such passive acceptance may lead you astray, away from the protection of family

and friends, or from your desired goals. Can you find your way home?

Ship
See **Boat**.

Shipwreck
A shipwreck in a dream may represent setbacks you are facing in life, in getting where you want to go—anything from feelings of failure or frustration to circumstances that are out of your control. If you wash up onto an island, the dream may be offering you a chance to start over.

Shoes (*See also* **Barefoot**.)
Your feet connect you to the earth—shoes in a dream may reflect that grounding (your attitudes and convictions) along with a sense of being protected. Removing your shoes may be a sign of respect. "If the shoe fits, wear it" may mean you need to accept a situation. Walking in someone else's shoes may give you a better understanding of, or greater compassion for, that person. Lastly, is it just possible that you're feeling the urge to go shopping?

Shopping (*See also* **Mall**.)
Shopping is very often a means to satisfy needs that you don't even know you have. True, it involves making decisions, knowing what's in fashion, and expressing your style—but it's still just buying. What are you buying in the dream and what purpose does it serve? If it merely takes up space—what space are you trying to fill?

Shovel (*See also* **Excavation**.)
A shovel is used to dig. Is the one in your dream digging something up from the past; is it digging a hole in which to bury something; or is it digging you out of trouble? A shovel can also clear away obstacles and prepare the earth for the planting of **Seeds**.

Shower
See **Bath**.

Signature
Your signature represents your identity. When you sign something, it usually means you give permission or make a contract. Giving someone your autograph is something else entirely. If it's someone else's signature, consider whose and what that person means to you.

Skin (*See also* **Acne**, **Injury**.)
Skin is a physical boundary; it provides protection from the envi-

ronment. In a dream, it may refer to feelings of separateness or concern about guarding your internal resources. It may also symbolize your degree of sensitivity (thick or thin skinned) or superficiality ("only skin deep"). The condition of your skin in the dream may represent feelings about your body or your physical appearance. Is something "getting under your skin"?

Sky (*See also* **Air**, **Cloud**.)

As the seat of heaven, the sky may represent transcendence, spirituality, and life after death. It is associated with cosmic consciousness, such questions as "What is the meaning of life?" A night sky may represent deeper (unconscious) issues.

Skyscraper

A skyscraper in your dream may represent your self, as a **House** does, and the elevation may give you a new perspective. Are you upwardly mobile or afraid of heights?

Sleeping

As odd as it may seem, a dream of being asleep may mean that something important in your life is not being acknowledged or understood; you may lack awareness. It may

point to sleep as an escape from reality; you may need to wake up and look around. Conversely, it may indicate peace of mind. If you are not getting enough rest, this dream may underscore the need for more.

Smoke (*See also* **Fire**.)

The smoke in your dream may be alerting you to a potentially dangerous situation ("where there's smoke, there's fire"). Smoke may also represent uncertainty or lack of clear vision.

Snail

Has your progress been too slow, or is it slow and steady ("slowly but surely")? The snail's shell may symbolize your external image. The snail may suggest that shyness is getting in the way of a more active social life.

Snake

Snakes symbolize healing (a staff bearing entwined snakes forms the caduceus, the symbol for the medical profession), rebirth and renewal (probably from the fact that

* Sleeping *

they shed their skin), and intuitive wisdom. More often in dreams, snakes are frightening. They may represent someone who is untrustworthy or devious, a "snake in the grass." They may symbolize temptation or a potentially poisonous friendship or situation.

Snow

Are you ready to get out of school and have some fun (snow days!) or anticipating a ski party? If not, this dream may be suggesting a clean start or something cold or frozen, perhaps feelings or a relationship.

Soup

Soup gives healing and nourishment, and in a dream, this may be in an emotional sense. The person who provides the soup may be someone who can help you. Soup also refers to a mess into which you may have gotten yourself (as in "in the soup").

Speech (*See also* **Talking**.)

If giving a speech in your dream, you may have something you want to communicate. Maybe you need to "tell it like it is." The dream may be processing anxiety about an upcoming report or oral presentation. If attending a speech, you may be learning something new.

Spider

In a dream, spiders may represent patience, creative power, healing, or helpfulness (think of Charlotte, who saved Wilbur from the butcher's block in *Charlotte's Web*). Spiders prey on pests such as mosquitoes and flies; perhaps you are trying to get rid of an annoyance. If the spider in your dream is frightening, the dream may be warning you of a trap or a sticky situation. A spider may also signify someone who manipulates others through intimidation or aggression.

Spider Web (*See also* **Maze**, **Spider**.)

If caught in a dream spider's web, you may be feeling somehow trapped. Perhaps some "little white lie" has grown into a tangled web of deceit. The web may also represent the spinning or weaving of your destiny. A spider's web shimmering with dew highlights the richness and delicacy of nature.

Spit

Is something "leaving a bad taste in your mouth"? Perhaps you need to spit it out. Spitting on someone indicates disrespect and disdain.

Square

The square is a symbol of wholeness, stability, and emotional balance. In dreaming of a square, your life may feel solid, fair, nourishing, and secure. If the square is broken or tilted, perhaps your life feels that way too. A square may also reflect a rigid attitude and strong determination to stick with convention.

Stain/Spot (*See also* **Bath**.)

A stain may represent something that feels dirty or soiled, or perhaps feelings of guilt or embarrassment. This dream may be a suggestion to wash out the spots.

Stairs

Stairs go both up and down; they may be dream symbols for ambition or a desire for (or a loss of) status or authority. Stairs may symbolize levels of awareness; you may be coming to a deeper understanding of something. In this light, stairs represent change and growth, as well as movement toward wholeness.

Star

A star may represent your hopes for the future—your goals and aspirations. This is the basis for the expressions to "reach for the stars" or to "follow your star." The expression "written in the stars" casts them as the forces of destiny.

As slang for a celebrity, a star draws admiration and attention. Traditionally, stars also offer spiritual guidance and hope. Stars are symbols of light in the darkness.

Stomach/Stomachache

The stomach dream may allude to something that makes you sick to your stomach, perhaps a change that you're having trouble accepting. Check out the possibility that it may reflect an actual illness or "stomach bug." A dream stomach may also suggest greed— your eyes may be "bigger than your stomach." The stomach is considered the seat of courage.

Storm

The dream storm may represent emotional turmoil or conflict, especially that which is hidden; it may be within you or in a relationship. Perhaps it is time to talk about and deal with the feelings, whether they be anger, frustration, or grief. Conversely, the storm may represent breaking through an emotion barrier and taking action.

Stranger

A stranger in a dream may represent an aspect of your self that is not well known or understood. A stranger may reflect qualities of

 Storm

other people or situations in your life. This dream may call your attention to some potentially dangerous belief, attitude, or person in your life.

Submarine

A submarine may represent adventure or a voyage. It suggests exploring the depths of your unconscious (as symbolized by **Water**) or your feelings. The sub offers safety and protection; it enables deep submersion with the power to ascend to the surface.

Suitcase

See **Luggage**.

Sun (*See also* **Heaven**, **Paradise**.)

The sun is the source of light and life. It means creative energy, awareness, and enlightenment. It is a symbol of intelligence, as opposed to intuition. A sunny day in your dream suggests feeling carefree, strong, or optimistic. Alternatively, it may represent a scorching heat from which you need shelter. Sunrise/sunset may signal the beginning or end of a phase in your life.

Swan

Maturing as it does from an ugly duckling, the graceful swan may be a symbol of patience, potential, and transformation. As it glides across the water, a swan is the very picture of serenity and beauty, which it also represents. Swans are symbols of family, as they mate for life and raise their young together.

Swearing

See **Oath**.

Swimming

In a dream, swimming through the **Water** (symbolic of your unconscious feelings and instincts) may represent trust and comfort in those aspects of your self. If you have difficulty swimming, you may have trouble dealing with your feelings; you may have to work to accept your self. If you are anxious in the water, you may have a problem facing your emotions or reservations about "jumping into" something. Swimming dreams also suggest relaxation and freedom. Of course, if you have a swim meet approaching, this dream may help you deal with the related anxieties and anticipation.

Sword (*See also* **Knight**, **Knife**.)

Unlike the knife, the sword has a majestic—even noble—quality, though it is similarly used for attack and defense. The sword may represent power, separation, the quest for truth, or protection against evil. A double-edged sword may hurt at the same time it helps.

T

Table

A table may refer to relationships with friends and family and your status in them (your place at the table). It may be that you need to bring something out into the open, to "lay it on the table." The table may represent feelings about some activity that occurs around a table (eating, a meeting). The table itself may not be central to the dream's meaning; consider the condition and construction of the table, the items on it, and the activity taking place around it.

Talking (*See also* **Speech**.)

Who or what is talking and what is being said? In legends and folklore, talking birds, plants, and animals often help or guide the **Hero**. If the speaker in your dream is something or someone unusual, consider your feelings about whom or what it might

represent and what it is saying. Difficulty talking in your dreams may relate to having trouble getting through to others.

Target (*See also* **Arrow**.)

A target may be your hopes or ambitions. Are you hitting the bull's-eye or are your shots going wild? If on target, you are focused and heading in the right direction. If you are the target of someone's anger, someone may be taking shots at you.

Tattoo

Tattoos originated as forms of initiation and physical adornment. They may represent allegiance or identification, or protection from danger. As always, consider related symbols: the image being tattooed, where, and onto whom. In a dream, a tattoo may suggest an experience that has somehow left its mark on you.

Taxi (*See also* **Car**.)

As a taxi passenger, you determine the destination, but you rely on someone else to get you there. This dream may deal with asking for help to find your way. Perhaps you feel as if you don't control your **Journey**. If you're doing the driving, you feel confident that you know the way and have the means to get where you want to go. This dream may be processing a recent, or planned, trip to the city.

Teacher (*See also* **Exam**.)

Teachers in dreams may offer advice or give guidance; a dream teacher may be a leader who steers you toward maturity and self-discipline. The real source of this apparent wisdom is your unconscious and the dream may concern your ability to trust your own advice. This dream may underscore feelings about a particular teacher or about school in general.

Tears

See **Crying**.

Teddy Bear (*See also* **Doll**.)

Does the teddy bear offer security and comfort? It may represent companionship and reassurance, or simply cuddling. It may symbolize a real teddy bear you once owned—or still do.

Teeth

Teeth symbolize strength, aggressiveness, greed, or an unjustified level of confidence. Have you bitten off more than you can chew? Dreams about teeth may deal with embarrassment ("losing face") or regret about having made a biting remark.

Losing teeth: These fairly common dreams point to transitions, such as the replacement of your lost baby teeth by adult ones as you mature. Your reaction to the dream may reflect your feelings about new roles and responsibilities. Dreams about losing adult teeth often concern appearance—making a good impression or being found attractive. Losing teeth in dreams may suggest talking too much or without thinking first.

Telephone (*See also* **Radio**.)

Have you ever been jolted out of bed by a ringing telephone only to discover that you dreamt the whole thing? This dream is literally trying to get you to wake up and pay attention. The call may be a direct line to your unconscious. Be sure to listen carefully.

A dream in which you're having difficulty connecting may be another wake-up call. It may signal a breakdown in communication with someone—the connection is being lost. Something may be threatening the relationship; a **Storm** may have knocked down the line.

Television

What you are watching may reflect your feelings. Is your dream TV a news source or a mindless diversion from more serious issues? Television is a passive means of "tuning in" to the world, but it also removes you from the story. This may enhance your understanding and give a more objective view, but it may also enable you to overlook disquieting issues by equating them with other TV stories, such as soap operas.

Tent

A dream involving a tent may deal with the outdoors, adventure, and nature. A tent (like a **House**) may represent the self—or a part of you that is temporary or unstable. Do you (or does anyone around you) tend to "pack up and go" at a moment's notice?

Test

See **Exam**, **Quiz**.

Theater (*See also* **Actor**, **Audience**, **Performance**.)

The scene onstage in the theater may be from your own life; consider how the action relates to it. The characters may represent some aspect of you and the way you present yourself to the world; this is a chance to view them from a different perspective. The theater is a symbol of ideals and ambitions. Are you wishing for your "moment on stage"? Conversely, this dream may be telling you not to be so dramatic.

Thief (*See also* **Burglar**.)

The thief may represent something that threatens to steal your energy or emotional strength. This dream may also deal with loss, specifically loss in a relationship.

Thirst

This dream may represent emotional or spiritual longings. You may feel in some way parched, lifeless, or wilted. Do you need **Water** (insight, energy, knowledge)? However, you may actually be thirsty. You may need to wake up and get a drink of water.

Thorn

The thorn may represent an obstacle or a difficult or tricky situation (a "thorny problem"). It may refer to unresolved pain that continues to keep you "stuck." It may be someone you know who is being a pain, a "thorn in your side."

Throne (*See also* **King**, **Queen**.)

Those who sit on thrones often represent power, authority, or justice; the dream may suggest your feelings about those qualities. You may seek recognition or an elevated status. If you are the power behind the throne, perhaps you have capabilities that are unrecognized.

Thunder (*See also* **Lightning**, **Storm**.)

Thunder may be the voice of the gods. Is it sending you a message? Thunder represents anger or emotional outburst. It may concern assertiveness (too much or too little) in expressing your feelings. A clap of thunder may herald the emergence of new strengths; thunder in a dream may suggest feeling intimidated, under attack, or overwhelmed.

Time (*See also* **Clock**.)

Dreams about time suggest finding balance. Do you have a deadline looming? Perhaps you need to set one for yourself. Or do you have too many? If time is standing still, your life, or some part of it, may feel stuck; conversely, you may need to slow down. If time flies by, you may be busy and productive; or you may be stressed out. The dream may refer to a specific time in your life or something that happened then. It may mean that *now* is the time (seize the day!).

Toilet (*See also* **Bathroom**.)

This dream image is often a symbol of relief, of having discharged an emotional or other burden. You may need to dump some anxiety, fear, or responsibility, or something shameful or embarrassing. A clogged or overflowing toilet may symbolize emotions that are bound up and overwhelming.

Tongue

The tongue is a symbol of language and communication, eloquence and persuasion—in short, the power of words. It may symbolize taste in the sense of eating **Food** or of "having good taste," being esthetically or intellectually discriminating. A tongue in a dream may indicate honest communication or the lack of it. A sharp tongue utters words that are biting or hurtful. If you are holding your tongue, you are being discreet. A forked tongue spreads lies or deceit.

Tornado

The tornado symbolizes a sudden and uncontrollable destructive force, possibly in the form of ideas, feelings, events, or relationships. Is there any such force in your life?

Towel

You may want to clean something up or wipe it away. Is there something you want to cover up and pretend never happened? If you "throw in the towel," you may feel like giving up.

Tower

A tower symbolizes power and materialism or hopes and dreams. It suggests issues of arrogance on the one hand and low self-esteem on the other. Are you in the tower looking down, or on the ground looking up? Attempting to climb a tower may represent lofty goals or reaching for greater spiritual insight. If you withhold your feelings (keep them captive in the tower), you may come across as cold or distant.

Train (*See also* **Railroad**.)

Taking a train is a way of reaching a destination. The track may be a symbol for your path through life. Missing a train may symbolize losing an opportunity. C.G. Jung felt that using public transport was a symbol for conformity, for allowing others (or society) to dictate personal behavior.

Trash

See **Garbage**.

Tree

A tree is a symbol of life, strength, wisdom, and endurance. It represents intellectual and spiritual maturity, balance, and completeness: it can reach for the heavens only so long as it is firmly rooted in the ground (reality). New foliage on a tree may symbolize hopefulness. Fruit on it may symbolize talents or abilities. A tree in winter or with dead or broken branches may point to feelings about a change in your life or a sense that a part of yourself is flawed. Branches on the tree may represent your family and your role in the family. Climbing a tree may symbolize adventure or a new perspective.

Trial (*See also* **Judge/Jury**.)

This dream generally relates to issues of judgment, responsibility, and guilt. What role do you play in the dream? If you are the accused, you may be feeling guilty or defensive. What is your crime? Perhaps you feel wronged (a victim) and want justice to be served. This dream may relate to the ability to make informed decisions. Do you need to be more accepting and less judgmental of yourself or others?

Triangle

The geometric expression of the number three, a triangle may represent the threefold nature of man (body/mind/spirit), the Holy Trinity (the Father/the Son/the Holy Ghost), or a love triangle.

Turtle

Turtles move slowly and deliberately; they retreat into their shells for defense. A dream of a turtle may deal with being (too) slow in some way; alternatively, it may demonstrate that "slow and steady wins the race." A turtle may symbolize withdrawing or hiding, perhaps to shelter a sensitive nature. Turtles enjoy very long lives. For this reason, they often symbolize health and immortality.

U

UFO (*See also* **Extraterrestrial**.)

A UFO in a dream may represent the quest for spiritual purpose and wholeness or the powers of creativity and imagination. A spaceship may also contain a part of your personality that feels "alienated" or "from outer space." Creative expression of this quality may enable you to reach new heights. Think about it.

Umbrella

An umbrella may protect you from life's storms (emotional cloudbursts). On the other hand, it keeps out the **Sun**—you may be avoiding new ideas or insights from your unconscious (**Water**).

Umpire

See **Referee**.

Underground

What is underground often represents the unconscious. This dream may introduce emotions or parts of your self that have been repressed—buried or willfully forgotten. Those that threaten you may appear as rodents, reptiles, or other unappealing figures. If you have no reservations about exploring your unconscious, you may see yourself underground exploring caves or mining for gold.

Underwear (*See also* **Nakedness**.)

Underwear may symbolize parts of your self, habits or prejudices, that you generally keep hidden. This may suggest shame or embarrassment about things you don't want others to see. Alternatively, the dream may signal acceptance or acknowledgment of a previously hidden part.

Undressing

See **Nakedness**.

Unicorn

The unicorn represents innocence and purity as the most wise and powerful of mythical beasts. In legend, the unicorn can counteract the effects of poison. The unicorn stands for power, imagination, and the resolution of conflict.

Uniform (*See also* **Disguise**.)

Wearing a uniform in a dream suggests issues of conformity, peer pressure, and self-awareness. Are you trying hard to be like everybody else? Alternatively, you may be too much the "rugged individual." A uniform represents connection to a group and a sense of community. If you wear a school uniform, this dream may relate to school.

Universe

The universe in dreams can represent issues from the cosmic to the mundane—from spiritual questions concerning the nature of life or your place in the world to your own feelings of insignificance.

Unlock (*See also* **Key**, **Lock**.)

This dream may represent a freeing of energies, ideas, or emotions; the loosening of boundaries or restrictions; or the exposing of secrets. It may concern the reverse: keeping these things under lock and key. Examine carefully whatever is being locked up or released in the dream.

Usher

The usher may be serving as a guide. Follow, and see what happens. You may just find your "proper place" in life.

V

Vacation

Maybe you need to unwind and take a break from your daily stress. If it's someone else on vacation, you may feel as if others are leaving you to do all the work while they take it easy. If you have trouble getting to the vacation spot or the vacation turns into a disaster, you may be too anxious or uptight really to let yourself go and relax.

Vacuum Cleaner

There may be "dirt" in some part of your life. Let this dream vacuum cleaner suck it up.

Vagabond (*See also* **Beggar**.)

Have you been wandering without a goal or destination? This dream may be encouragement to settle down and find a home. It may suggest that help is needed in your search for adventure or for answers.

Valentine

This dream often comes around February 14th, when you may be wondering who might or might not give you a valentine. Are you thinking about whether you should send one to someone special?

Valley

As much as a valley may represent security, fertility, and deepening knowledge, descending into one may symbolize depression or a low point in your life, or feelings of isolation. The mountains that border the valley may be barriers, but you can scale them.

Vampire

The vampire in dreams may signify feelings or thoughts you have tried to shut out of your mind; you may be unconscious of them, but they can drain your energy all the same. Try to bring them into the light. The vampire may represent a person or situation that is overly demanding ("sucking the life out of you"). Make sure your friends are positive influences and aren't just using you to get something. If you are the vampire, you may need to discover your passions and goals so that you can take constructive steps to achieve them. No one else can truly satisfy your needs or desires.

Veil (*See also* **Mask**.)

The veil may cover something secret or hidden; lifting the veil means disclosing it. Is it something you are concealing or revealing? The veil may symbolize mourning, modesty, protection, or ignorance.

Velvet

Luxury characterizes velvet; at the same time, it's sensuous and comfortable. It's always appropriate for a formal occasion, for "black tie." Black velvet may also be worn in mourning.

Victim

If you are the victim in the dream, it may reflect your having been hurt or taken advantage of in real life; it may refer to feelings of self-hatred. Consider whether this role is somewhat familiar to you. It may be time to stand up for yourself, or even fight back. Victimizing someone else may express anger, just as it exerts control. Examine who or what you are victimizing and for what reason.

Victory

Victory represents success and it comes in many forms. The most satisfying may be your personal triumphs, when succeeding means overcoming your doubts or fears. Other victories involve competition, battling an enemy, breaking through a barrier, or finishing a project. All are thrilling achievements. If you have an upcoming competition, this dream may be mental practice and preparation. It may also signal your increasing ability to succeed, to win in life.

Video Game

Consider the role video games play in your life and what games you are playing in the dream. Video games offer diversion and vicarious thrills. At the same time, they provide escape from responsibility and social interaction. They are a poor substitute for real-life experience. Do the games provide such an escape in your dream, or are you merely reliving the vivid images from earlier in the day?

Vine

A vine may represent the flow of nourishment and energy for growth, yet it has a tendency to entangle and to cling. A grapevine may represent the exchange of gossip or rumor.

Violin

As does all musical symbolism, this dream may allude to harmony or discord. String instruments in particular may refer to tension. The fiddle has its own associations with the culture of country music and blue grass. In mythology, the fiddle has magical properties. Like all such dreams, this one may refer to actual experience with the

Violin

violin or anticipation of an upcoming performance.

Vitamin

Do you need more energy? This dream may deal with issues of health or nutrition.

Volcano

A volcanic eruption may represent an uncontrolled release of emotion or energy. Have you (or has someone around you) been letting off steam destructively? Perhaps a little restraint is needed.

Vomiting (*See also* **Stomach/ Stomachache**.)

Vomiting is a very effective way to eliminate something you can't "stomach," even unpleasant feelings. Such a dream may symbolize a dumping of guilt, anxiety, or hostility. Could the dream relate to any eating habits you practice?

Vulture

As scavengers, vultures clean the bones of dead animals; they can be said to live off the misfortune of others. Is someone likewise picking on you; do you exploit the weaknesses of others? The vulture is associated with danger and with the seeking of opportunities in unlikely or undesirable places.

W

Wagon

A wagon may be similar to a **Car** as a means of transportation and symbol of your self, but it is more often a symbol of life change or transition. You may be pulling a heavy load, hauling a lot of problems; the wagon may just as well hold things that will help you along the way.

Waiter/Waitress

The waiter or waitress in your dream may symbolize helpfulness or service. You may want to serve or to be served. If, as in dreams about **Food**, you are awaiting nourishment, the server may be offering to help restore your energy or health.

Waiting

This dream may refer to anxiety about test results or excitement about something you're looking forward to. It may deal with the frustrations inherent in growing up. It may even be suggesting that you put your worries on hold.

Walking

Walking in a dream may be a metaphor for how you are making your way through life. If you are moving along at a good pace, you are performing effectively. If you limp or stumble, you may be facing obstacles in getting where you want to go. Walking alone may mean independence or a desire to "go it alone," but it may also suggest loneliness. Walking with others may mean that you enjoy the help and company of friends.

Wall

In dreams, a wall may symbolize an obstacle; if you are climbing the wall, it is an obstacle you are over-coming. Walls provide defense, safety, and protection, but they can confine and isolate at the same time. Be sure you aren't putting up walls when you need to be open with your feelings and willing to let others in. Alternatively, you may occasionally need to set limits and protect yourself by saying no. Walls set boundaries and give privacy. The trick is to know when to build them and how high.

Wand

A magic wand concentrates and directs energy. You may want more control over a situation or a magical solution to a problem. If the wand is directed at you, something (or someone) may have you spellbound.

War

Dreams of war may be metaphors for your own conflicting beliefs, ideas, or feelings (being at war with yourself). War dreams may reflect the reality of parents who are fighting or a fight you are having with a sibling or friend. They may also stem from a real or threatened war or from fighting in general. If you have these dreams often, it may help to talk with someone about them.

Warehouse

A warehouse holds things in storage, so take an honest look at the symbolism of the items being stored; they may be resources, talents, ambitions. If the objects are being hoarded however, you may be trying to fill an emptiness you feel inside. Is the warehouse empty? If so, perhaps your energy is running low. If the warehouse is eerie or spooky, this may be similar to a **Chase** dream.

Warmth (See also **Fever**.)

Warmth is associated with good feelings, comfort and cuddling, relaxing saunas, and steam or sunbaths. This dream may also signal an actual change in room (or your body) temperature.

Warrior

A warrior is trained in close combat, in the skills of defense and attack. In a dream, he may symbolize the working through of some inner conflict. Are you dealing with righteous anger or simply an urge to fight?

Washing (*See also* **Bath**.)

Washing is a common symbol for cleansing and purification. You may be washing away something obsolete or undesirable. Is there anything in your life that feels dirty or no longer useful? A stain that won't come out may point to guilt; washing hands denotes innocence.

Watch

See **Clock**, **Time**.

Water (*See also* **Bath**, **Drowning**, **Flood**, **Ocean**, **River**, **Swimming**.)

It is water in which life began. As a dream symbol, therefore, it represents things basic and far-reaching: the emotions; the unconscious; energy; fertility; knowledge; spirituality; in short, the essence of life. Water is a symbol of change and the ability to be transformed. In what form does the water appear—a river, an ocean, a pond, a flood, or a glass half full? And what is its condition—stormy and raging or placid and smooth, crystal clear or muddy? The water in your dream may indicate your feelings about something, whether those feelings are gentle and calm or fierce and overwhelming.

Waterfall

A waterfall may represent an outpouring of energy; it may be a sign that you are "going with the flow." If you dream you are about to tumble over a waterfall, it may signify anxiety about something potentially dangerous, perhaps even an overwhelming rush of emotion.

Wealth (*See also* **Money**.)

Dreams of wealth may deal with financial issues, but more often they are about your inner resources. The message may be that your personal qualities are your greatest wealth. Real treasure is a thing that money can't buy.

Weapon (*See also* **Cannon**, **Knife**.)

A weapon in a dream represents emotion, likely hidden or unexpressed, that is directed at yourself or others; it may be anger, fear, resentment, or internal conflict. Whatever the feeling, it's important to acknowledge it and find a way to channel it constructively.

sent wasted energy that may halt or retard more beneficial growth. In a dream, they may symbolize those qualities. Is there anything in your life that calls for weeding out, perhaps an idea or a relationship that slows your growth? "Weeds" may be gossip that can obscure the truth.

Werewolf
See **Wolf**.

Whale
The whale lives under **Water**, the unconscious, but must come to the surface to breathe; it may represent intuition bringing insights from your unconscious to your conscious mind. The whale also symbolizes the beauty and enormity of nature and the danger of its extinction. A whale is symbolic of a great responsibility, or of being overwhelmed by one, much like Jonah or Pinocchio, who were swallowed whole. Are you running from something you must do?

Wedding (*See also* **Marriage**.)
A wedding in a dream may not be what it seems—it may stem from changes you experience as the parts of your personality come together as a balanced whole. A dream wedding may represent feelings about relationships, security, or home; it may suggest concerns about your parents' marriage. If you are going to be in a wedding, this dream may be anticipating the event. And if you have a crush on someone, the message is pretty clear, isn't it?

Weeding/Weeds
Weeds grow in defiance of the most careful and diligent gardener to give the garden a look of disorder and neglect. They repre-

Wheelchair (*See also* **Disability**.)
If you are in the wheelchair, it may mean that you feel somehow restricted or confined. Are you letting other people push you around? It may be time to stand up for yourself. The dream may also

mean that you are learning to move forward again after dealing with a crippling problem. This dream may be challenging you to get going and stand on your own two feet. If someone else is in the wheelchair, that person may represent a part of yourself that you have unconsciously immobilized.

Whistle

A whistle draws attention, whether it be signaling impending danger or hailing a **Taxi**. It may even show personal interest, as in a "wolf whistle." It may be a signal, like a bell, to begin or end an activity. Is there something you need to stop or start doing? Consider how the whistle is used in the dream. Someone who is carefree and light-hearted may whistle a happy tune.

White

Associations with the color white are peace, purity, completeness, perfection, idealism, innocence, and newness. White is the color of fresh knowledge and aware-ness and the seeking of spiritual holiness. In folktales, a white animal often lures a person away from ordinary life into adven-ture. Consider how the color is used in your dream and what feelings it evokes.

Wig (*See also* **Baldness**, **Disguise**, **Hair**, **Mask**.)

In a dream, a wig symbolizes deception or artificiality. It may hint at lying or suggest a change in the way you present yourself to people. Have you been disguising some part of your self? A dream wig may cover something about which you feel shame or embar-rassment. Wig dreams may also deal with anxieties about illness, hair loss, or the loss of power or esteem.

Wild Animal (*See also* **Animal**.)

This dream often resembles a **Chase** dream in which you run from something scary. Examine the symbolism of the animal in the dream. The animal itself (or its qualities) may characterize someone in your life or some part of your personality. A dream in which you run from the wild animal, but later subdue and control it, usually signifies your ability to cope with whatever the animal represents.

Wind

The wind may symbolize emotions; intellect; life force, spirit, or energy; or change. It may be a force creative or destructive, depending on its strength. A gentle wind can carry

Seeds (ideas and insights) to start new growth. But a heavy gale can cause havoc. How hard is the wind blowing in your dream and in which direction? Keep in mind that wind direction changes often and very quickly.

Window

The window may represent your outlook on life and your awareness of what is going on around you. Is the window clean and sparkling or smudged and dirty? If you are looking out of a window, you may need a new perspective on the situations or people around you. If you are looking in, perhaps you need to take a closer look at yourself or shift your point of view.

Winter (*See also* **Ice**, **Snow**.)

Winter is the season of rest (sleep) before the next cycle of growth (awakening) in spring. In a dream, it may suggest that your feelings are cooling or on hold about a person or situation. Winter may symbolize old age and decline, or it may just reflect enjoyment of snow and winter sports.

Wise Old Man/ Wise Old Woman

These figures are archetypes (the original patterns or models on which all similar ideas are based) that represent spirituality and wisdom. Pay careful attention to their words. It may be your unconscious speaking through them, offering guidance or insight of extreme value to your growth and happiness.

Wolf

Like all animals, a wolf is driven by cravings and instincts. Wolves are loners; when gathered in a pack, however, they are loyal and cooperative. A crafty predator, the wolf may symbolize greed or hunger. In a dream, a wolf will have these same associations. Are you a lone wolf? Do you run in a pack? Is there some powerful devouring force or person in your life?

Wood (*See also* **Forest**, **Tree**.)

Wood is a natural material from which countless things are made. It is held by some to retain the vital energy that once made it a living tree. At the same time, "wooden" is a way of acting that is stiff and without emotion. Working with wood is a creative act in cooperation with nature.

Wool

Wool is a natural fiber that protects against cold. Lamb's wool is packed into the toes of a ballet slipper to cushion a dancer's foot. As a symbol, wool suggests a simple life, a gentle nature, or anything smooth, soft, and dense like the coat of a sheep. "Woolgathering" is an expression meaning daydreaming. If someone "pulls the wool over your eyes," they are trying to trick you.

Worm

The worm is a lowly creature residing **Underground**, operating on blind instinct. In a dream, it may represent a person or thing that is coarse, insignificant, or contemptible. Are you trying to worm your way out of something? The worm also symbolizes earth and earthiness. Earthworms are friends to the gardener, as they mulch the soil and improve it. Likewise, in a dream they may turn up and enrich the soil (your mind), making it more fertile and productive.

Wreck (*See also* **Accident**.)

A car wreck in a dream may suggest concerns about something dangerous. Are you acting recklessly? Are you afraid of losing control? If you have seen or been involved in a wreck, this dream may tap into memories of it.

Wrestling

In a wrestling match, two opponents grapple, struggling against each other for a win. This dream may symbolize a conflict within you. Who or what is your opponent? What is your attitude? This may be an indication of how you tackle your problems in waking life. Of course, this dream may be unconscious preparation for a real wrestling match.

Writing

Writing is a way of thinking on paper—of sorting, organizing, and clarifying ideas—that leads to understanding. In a dream, writing is probably symbolic of communication or self-expression. Regardless of who is writing in the dream, it may be a message from your inner self, and it may contain useful insight.

X

X

X is the symbol for an intersection or crossroad; it may relate to a decision you're considering. An X is commonly used to indicate a spot on a map, usually either "you are here" or a destination. On a

X-ray

treasure map, an X may symbolize the hidden wealth of your unique talents and abilities. It is also the "signature" of someone who is unable to write or who wants to remain anonymous. Don't overlook the possibility that the dream X is the Roman numeral 10 or that it indicates multiplication, perhaps even the expansion of your unfolding awareness.

X-ray

Dreaming of an X-ray suggests you may be feeling exposed or vulnerable, or that you have arrived at some new insight. Can people see through you or your **Mask**? You may be seeing through a lie. This dream may also relate to the actual experience of having an X-ray taken.

Y

Yard

A yard may represent a child's world, an area where children can play in safety. In a dream, it may suggest your own boundaries, the personal limits you set in your relationships with others. What is the condition of the yard? If it needs to be mowed or **Weed**ed, you may have some work to do on yourself.

A broken or sagging **Fence** may call attention to ineffective or failing boundaries.

Yardstick

A dream yardstick may symbolize the standards you set for yourself. Do you "measure up"? You may be too much a perfectionist—or you may be slacking and coming up short. How much are you asking of yourself? If you are working on a project, perhaps you need to be more exacting.

Yeast

Yeast may represent a thing seemingly small and insignificant that has the potential to change— possibly even transform—everything. An energy or idea may be developing.

Yelling

Consider the circumstances in which you yell: when other noise drowns you out; when others are not listening; when you express a lot of emotional energy. In a dream, it suggests one of these conditions. You may feel strongly, like excitement at a ball game or anger and frustration; you may be calling for help. Do any of these circumstances apply to you?

Yellow

Yellow is associated with the sun, light, and **Gold**. It may symbolize energy, happiness, peace, or intelligence. More muddy shades may represent cowardice, caution (a yellow stoplight), or irritableness.

Youth

See **Child**.

Zero

Zero in a dream may point to nothingness or insignificance; it may signify low self-esteem or emotional emptiness. Your life or your future may feel meaningless or trivial, but the circle shape may also represent wholeness and perfection. "Zero hour" may be an important deadline, perhaps for a big project or decision.

Zipper

A zipper is a handy means of access into things ranging from handbags to jackets. Zippers may relate to feelings about **Nakedness** or exposing your feelings and beliefs, and hearing those of others. A zipper in a dream may be suggesting that you "zip your lip." A broken zipper may point to frustration in finishing a project...or a problem with your wardrobe.

Zoo

In dreams, animals often represent instinctive urges and intuition; the conditions in the zoo may reflect how you feel about this part of your self. The zoo may suggest emotional chaos or a lack of discipline ("the place is a zoo"). Or could you just be enjoying an excursion?

Sleep Habits

For one week, keep track of when you go to bed, what time you wake up, whether you feel rested, and any problems you have falling asleep, waking up or during the night. This will help you see patterns in your sleep habits and aid in dream recall. Make a separate entry for each day and include the following information: bedtime; the time you fell asleep; the time you awaken; and notes about how you slept.

Dream Journaling

Use the suggestions below as a starting point for keeping your very own dream journal. If you jot down your dreams every morning (or every couple of mornings), you will begin to remember your dreams more easily and understand better what they mean. Remember to note the date and time that you make the entries into your journal.

1. What I was thinking about before I fell asleep

2. My feelings when I first woke up

3. The dream

4. Important actions or elements in the dream (e.g., falling, a man, a star)

5. What I think the dream might mean

Dream Exercise 3

Interpreting Your Dreams

As you continue to journal your dreams, break out the different parts so that you can begin to understand how the dream may relate to your waking life. Keep in mind that your dreams filter through your waking experience—the occurrences, people, and ideas you deal with every day. The definitions in *The Girls' Guide to Dreams* will suggest the possible meanings of certain symbols but they are only a starting point. The meaning of your dream is unique to you.

To help explore that meaning, consider the following questions and enter your thoughts about them into your dream journal.

1. Where did the dream take place (inside or out, city or country, a particular room in a house, someplace familiar or unknown)?

2. What time/season/year is it in the dream?

3. Were there people in the dream? Who were they?

4. Were there any animals in the dream? What kind of animals were they?

5. What happened in the dream?

6. What was said in the dream?

7. How did you feel in the dream?

8. Did anything that happened in the dream seem familiar from your daily life?

9. How did the dream end (what was the "solution" to the dream)?

10. How might this dream relate to your everyday life?

Dream Exercise 4
Dream Animals

Copy the list of animals below into your dream journal, leaving a blank space next to each one. Then jot down a word in each of the blank spaces. Don't think about it—just write down the first word that pops into your head.

Alligator	Donkey	Mole	Snake
Ant	Elephant	Mouse	Spider
Bat	Fish	Octopus	Swan
Bear	Fox	Ostrich	Tiger
Bird	Frog	Owl	Turtle
Butterfly	Giraffe	Parrot	Unicorn
Camel	Gorilla	Peacock	Vulture
Cat	Hippopotamus	Porcupine	Walrus
Caterpillar	Horse	Rabbit	Whale
Cow	Insect	Raccoon	Whale
Dinosaur	Leopard	Rat	Worm
Dog	Lizard	Shark	Zebra
Dolphin	Lion	Sheep	

Now that you have thought about these areas of your life and examined what you think and feel about various animals, you will have some idea of what they may symbolize in your dreams. The important thing in interpreting your dreams is to understand the meaning of each individual symbol to you. Use this same exercise for other symbols—people, places, things, even situations—to figure out what you think and feel about them and what they may mean in your dreams.

Dream Exercise
5
Everyday Life

This exercise has you brainstorm about parts of your life that may show up in your dreams—the things you think about and the way you feel about them. Some suggestions are given below. What's happening in these areas? Does it cause anxiety, create excitement, prolong suspense? Is there anything you'd like to change? Jot down in your dream journal whatever comes fairly quickly to mind.

Friends	Spiritual life
Family	Future
School	I need help with....
Health	I worry about....
Appearance	I am happiest when....
Sports	I hate it when....
Extracurricular activities/clubs	I wish....

Index

Note: Index includes topics not already alphabetized in Alphabetical Listings of symbols on pages 8-122.